LEGAL AND CONTRACTUAL PROCEDURES FOR ARCHITECTS

FIFTH EDITION

BOB GREENSTREET
DAVID CHAPPELL
MICHAEL DUNN

with additional material

by

Karen Greenstreet

Architectural Press

OXFORD AMSTERDAM BOSTON LONDON NEW YORK PARIS
SAN DIEGO N FRANCISCO SINGAPORE SYDNEY TOKYO

Architectural Press
An imprint of Elsevier Science
Linacre House, Jordan Hill, Oxford OX2 8DP
200 Wheeler Road, Burlington MA 01803

First published 1981
Second edition 1984
Third edition 1989
Fourth edition 1994
Fifth edition 2003

British Library Cataloguing in Publication Data
A catalogue record for this book is available from the British Library

Library of Congress Cataloguing in Publication Data
A catalogue record for this book is available from the Library of Congress

ISBN   0 7506 5408 2

For information on all Architectural Press publications visit our website at
www.architecturalpress.com

Typset by Keyword Typesetting Services Ltd
Printed and bound in Great Britain

CONTENTS

PREFACE

In everyday practice, the architect spends considerable time carrying out various administrative tasks and dealing with problems and situations arising from the design and construction of each new building project. In order to do this effectively, a basic knowledge of all relevant procedures involved is necessary, coupled with an understanding of the broader legal and professional issues that are at stake.

Legal and Contractual Procedures for Architects provides a comprehensive, concise and simplified source of practical information, giving the reader a basic legal overview of the wider principles affecting the profession, and concentrating on the more specific procedural aspects of the architect's duties. In addition, it contains a series of checklists, diagrams and completed forms which provide a quick and easy reference source.

Each section of the book culminates with a number of problems that could face the architect, laid out on 'action required' sheets. These are dealt with in the context of a simulated office scenario on the following 'action taken' pages, where (to facilitate easy reading) an office diary format has been adopted. The responses on these pages are not meant to be model answers, as each problem would in reality merit its own unique handling. Rather, they are meant to convey an *attitude* appropriate to successful practice management. Students preparing for Part III RIBA examinations are advised to work through the book, attempting the problems themselves before checking their answers against those in the text.

The 1998 Edition *Standard Form of Building Contract* (Private with Quantities) has been referred to throughout, and a commentary of its Conditions is included on pages 54 to 57. Also, many of the forms used in the book are published by the RIBA; although their use is not mandatory, they are useful in providing a consistency of understanding for all parties involved in the construction process, and are therefore recommended in most cases.

Legal and Contractual Procedures for Architects offers only a basic framework of information, as a detailed coverage of the numerous aspects of the subject could not possibly be crammed into 108 pages. For this reason, the text is carefully cross-referenced to other sources, both at the foot of each page, and in the final section. Lack of space has also dictated that certain matters (e.g. work in public organisations) have been excluded.

Since the original publication of this book in 1981, there have been numerous changes in the legal, professional and administrative aspects of architecture. In consequence, a second edition was published in 1984 which substantially updated and enlarged the original text which was again revised in the third edition, published in 1989. The fourth edition, published in 1994, has now been revised, and every attempt has been made to respond to further developments of the past eight years.

Our thanks go to the following:

RIBA for permission to use their documents.

KAREN GREENSTREET MA PhD SOLICITOR for considerable assistance in the preparation of the original text, including much of the legal content, editing, referencing and indexing.

IAN FEWTRELL-SMITH RIBA DipArch (Oxford) for preparation of the standard forms and checking the text in the first edition.

JOHN CANE LLB DipArch (Birmingham) RIBA FFB FCIArb FFAS for contributions to the 'action required' and 'action taken' pages.

It is not the intention of the authors to provide a legal service in the publication of this book, but to offer an introduction to legal and practical matters concerning architecture. Legal assistance is advised where appropriate.

THE ARCHITECT AND THE LAW

Contents

Legal
Background

The Law

Law

English Law is basically a body of rules aimed at preserving the fabric of society, and is embodied in:

    COMMON LAW
    EQUITY
    LEGISLATION

Common law

The basic 'rules' of society have developed through the common law, and are governed by the doctrine of *stare decisis*, constraining English judges to stand by past decisions of superior courts. Although decisions must be based on the law decided in previous cases, the judge may draw relevant distinctions pertinent to each new case, enabling the common law to continually develop and adapt to the changing values of society. However, where a conflict arises between the common law and a statue, the latter prevails.

Equity

Equity provides a measure of fairness or natural justice not always available under statute or common law, by allowing additional remedies and procedures based on principles of 'conscience' to supplement the law.

Legislation

Legislation is written or enacted law passed or introduced by Parliament or a body whose authority derives from Parliament.

Acts or statutes are the principal means by which Parliament passes laws. They are suggested by concerned parties (often a government minister), prepared and laid before both the House of Lords and House of Commons in the form of a Bill and, if approved, become Acts of Parliament. In some cases, an Act may serve as enabling legislation, empowering more specific requirements to be made in the form of Rules, Orders or Statutory Instruments. For example, the Building Act 1984 empowers the creation of Building Regulations 1985 (as amended) and the Building Regulations 2001 as Statutory Instruments.

From a more practical standpoint, law can be classified into two branches:

    CRIMINAL LAW
    CIVIL LAW

Criminal law

This is public law, concerned with offences against the state (society) as a whole, e.g. robbery, murder, theft. Crimes may also be acts which, although not anti-social in a moral sense, infringe rules existing to ensure the smooth administration of the country, e.g. tax offences, certain road traffic offences. Most crimes are now covered by statutes, although several common law offences still exist.

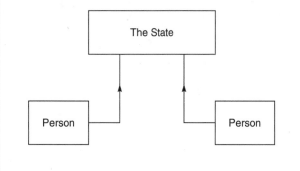

Civil law

This is private law, concerned with the rights and obligations of individuals and corporations in their dealings with each other. It is frequently embodied in the general common law although there is an increasing tendency to enact civil law provisions, e.g. Misrepresentation Act 1967, Unfair Contract Terms Act 1977.

    Matters covered by civil law provisions include:

        SUCCESSION
        FAMILY
        CONTRACT
        TORT
        PROPERTY
        EMPLOYMENT

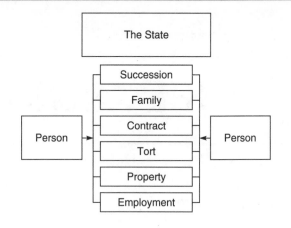

Contract and tort

To architectural practice, the most relevant branches of civil law are:

- contract law, which concerns the legally binding rights and obligations of parties who have made an agreement for a specific purpose (see page 51), and
- tort, literally a 'wrong' done by one individual or corporation to another for which a remedy (e.g. compensation, injunction) may be sought. There are a number of specific torts. These include:

    NEGLIGENCE (see page 4)
    TRESPASS (see page 35)
    NUISANCE
    DEFAMATION

It is possible that an action may fall under both the law of contract and tort (where, for example, a negligent act results in a breach of contract). In such a case it is sometimes easier to sue under the contract, rather than prove the tort.

References

LAW, pp. 1–39.
ARCHITECT'S LEGAL HANDBOOK, pp. 3–6.

The courts

For purposes of administrative expediency, different types of legal questions are dealt with in different courts. There is a wide variety of specialist courts designed to provide an efficient means of disposing of specific matters. These include:
- The Coroner's Court
- Employment Appeal Tribunal
- The Restrictive Practices Court

However, the courts which deal with the majority of cases in England and Wales are:
- The County Courts
- The High Court
- The Magistrates' Courts
- The Crown Courts

The relationship and hierarchies within the criminal and civil court structures can be best illustrated in diagram form:

Criminal court

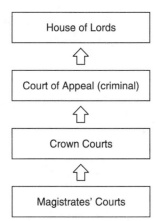

All criminal proceedings begin (and usually end) in the magistrates' court. However, more serious offences are always passed on to be tried in the crown courts.

Civil court

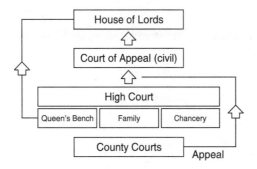

Proceedings in civil law may begin in either the county court or the High Court, depending
a) on the type of matter and
b) on the financial amount involved
Generally, the less financially consequential cases are heard in the county courts.

Appeal from the county court is not via the High Court, but directly to the Court of Appeal. In all civil court proceedings, legal representation is advisable, though not always strictly necessary.

Standard of proof

This is higher in criminal proceedings than in civil cases. In the former, the prosecution must prove its case against the defendant 'beyond a reasonable doubt'. Whereas in civil matters, the plaintiff bears the burden of proving allegations on the 'balance of probabilities'.

Other means available for the resolution of disputes include:
- ARBITRATION (see page 96)
- ADJUDICATION (see page 99)
- MEDIATION (see page 96)
- CONCILIATION (see page 96)
- SPECIAL TRIBUNALS, which tend to be less formal than the courts, and may be set up to reconcile individuals' rights with statutory demands enacted ostensibly to give them protection.

Small claims

Less formal procedures exist for individuals wishing to sue for sums less than £1,000 for personal injury claims and £5,000 for other claims in the county court. Small claims can be dealt with within the county court structure (the Small Claims Track). Legal representation is not necessary and the facts of the case are considered usually (but not always) by a district judge. The main advantage of the small claims procedure is that it enables anyone to sue for a relatively small amount without incurring legal costs which otherwise might easily exceed the amount of the claim. The claim should require only minimal preparation for the final hearing. For example, cases would not normally involve difficult points of law or numerous witnesses.

There are limits on the costs a winning party can recover, including those where an expert witness is necessary, e.g. a car mechanic.

In most legal matters affecting architectural practice, it is advisable to take legal advice before proceeding. There are various sources available:
> A SOLICITOR
> THE LOCAL LAW CENTRE
> CITIZEN'S ADVICE BUREAU

Legal aid may be available in civil matters, but only at the discretion of the regional administration of the Legal Aid Fund. Eligibility is dependent upon an individual's disposable income and capital.

References

THE SMALL CLAIMS TRACK (available from all county courts)
LAW, pp. 41–68, 69–74.

The Architect's Liability

The architect's legal obligations and responsibilities are governed by both statute and common law:

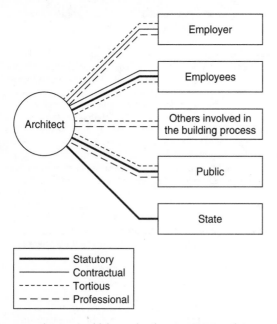

Architect → Employer, Employees, Others involved in the building process, Public, State

—————— Statutory
—————— Contractual
- - - - - - Tortious
— — — Professional

However, the areas which require the greatest attention are:
- breach of contract
- negligence

Breach of contract

The architect is not a party to the Standard Form of Building Contract (JCT 98), but has a separate contractual relationship with the employer (see page 27). In this, the architect agrees to carry out the work with reasonable skill and care. Failure to meet these standards will be in breach of the contract and if it results in problems causing extra expense or delays, the architect will be liable for damages.

Negligence

Outside the discernible contractual obligations imposed by the contract exists a duty under the law of torts (see page 2), particularly in negligence. The architect may be liable for the consequences arising from negligent behaviour, even where no contractual relationship exists.

The extent to which anyone may be held liable to others in tort depends on the DUTY OF CARE that is owed. In contractual situations, the liability of both parties is defined, but in tort, it is often difficult to determine the existence or extent of the duty of care. However, the law provides some guidance in certain circumstances by defining certain liabilities. The more important of these include:
> STRICT LIABILITY
> OCCUPIER'S LIABILITY
> EMPLOYER'S LIABILITY
> VICARIOUS LIABILITY

A. Strict

This applies in certain cases where liability may exist independently of wrongful intent or negligence. An illustration of this rule exists in *RYLANDS v FLETCHER 1968*, where water from a reservoir flooded the mineshaft on neighbouring property and led to a successful claim for damages, although no negligent act was proved. The decision against the reservoir owner was made on the basis that he had kept on his land 'something likely to do mischief', and that it had subsequently 'escaped'. Strict liability can also arise under statute, e.g. Control of Pollution Act 1974.

B. Occupier's

Under the Occupier's Liability Act 1957, an occupier of premises owes a duty of care to all lawful visitors to those premises. Under the Occupier's Liability Act 1984 an occupier owes certain duties to unlawful visitors to premises.

C. Employer's

An employer may be liable for injury caused to his or her employees by acts of negligence of fellow employees acting in the course of their employment. Liability also exists if the employer breaches his or her statutory duty, or if the injury is caused by the employer's negligence.

D. Vicarious

This may exist in certain limited circumstances where one party becomes responsible for certain acts of another without necessarily contributing to the negligence. The most common example of vicarious liability is an employer's responsibility for the acts of his or her employees.

Regarding responsibility to third parties, certain conditions must be shown to allow a claim for negligent behaviour to be successful. It must be shown:
- that a duty of care to the injured party existed at the time of the injury;
- that there was a breach of this duty;
- that the injured party suffered damage or loss as a result of the breach.

Standard of Care

In all cases, it is the REASONABLE STANDARD OF CARE established by common law against which a defendant party's performance will be judged.

> Liability based in negligence is not necessarily blameworthiness. It means falling short of a court's fixed standards, often a standard of perfects. Negligence is an arbitrary and uncertain concept.
>
> *Lord Monkman in HEDLEY BYRNE & CO. LTD v HELLER & PARTNERS LTD [1964]*

An examination of relevant caselaw on the following pages will give an indication of the position of the architect in relation to potentially hazardous areas in the duties where negligent behaviour has been determined. Note that liability in negligence is more restricted since the decision in Murphy v Brentwood District Council (1990) (see page 5)

References

LAW, pp. 174–229
ARCHITECT'S LEGAL HANDBOOK, pp. 309–43

1

HEDLEY BYRNE & CO. LTD v HELLER & PARTNERS LTD [1963] 2 All ER 575

- The Facts:
  A bank enquired on behalf of a customer whether, in the opinion of certain merchant bankers (the defendants) a company, E. Ltd, was of good financial status. The merchant bank replied that E. Ltd was respectably constituted, and good for its normal business engagements. The appellants relied upon these statements and subsequently suffered loss of over £17,000 as a result of E. Ltd becoming bankrupt.
- Held:
  Where in the ordinary course of business or professional affairs a person's skill or judgement is relied upon, and that person chooses to give information or advice without clearly showing that he or she does not accept responsibility, that person accepts a legal duty to exercise such care as the circumstances require in making a reply. If the person fails to exercise that degree of care, an action for negligence will lie if damage results.
- Comment:
  Prior to this case, it was thought that a person could be liable for negligent deeds, but not for negligent words. The principle of negligent misstatement arising out of Hedley Byrne was reiterated in Clay v A.J. Crump & Sons [1963] – where an architect, while inspecting a site in the course of demolition, negligently stated that a certain wall was safe and could remain. Subsequently, the wall collapsed causing injury to a labourer, and as a result the architect was held liable for his negligent misstatement.
  There is one notable exception to the general rule laid down in Hedley Byrne: a barrister is not liable for negligent advocacy, even where the client suffers loss through actual misstatements of the law (Rondel v Worsley [1967]). Hedley Byrne has been recently applied, but strictly interpreted in Caparo Industries plc v Dickman [1990].

2

MURPHY v BRENTWOOD DISTRICT COUNCIL [1990] 50 BLR 1

- The Facts:
  A housing estate was constructed in 1969 and the plaintiff bought one of a pair of semi-detached houses from the contractor in 1970. The concrete raft foundation design had been submitted to the Council. They had taken the advice of independent consulting engineers who recommended approval. The raft was subject to differential settlement causing cracking to the walls of the house and fracturing of a water pipe. The plaintiff was obliged to sell the house for considerably less than would have been its value if free from defects. The plaintiff brought an action for damages against the Council who were held liable to the plaintiff in negligence. An appeal to the Court of Appeal was dismissed and the Council appealed to the House of Lords.
- Held:
  – Negligence which results in a defect in the building itself is not actionable in tort.
  – In order to be actionable, the defect must cause damage to property other than the defective property or it must result in death or personal injury.
  – If the defect is discovered before it has caused any damage the cost of remedying the defect is not recoverable. There may be an exception if the defective structure is so close to the boundary as to pose a danger to other property after the defect is discovered.
  – It is not permissible to consider a structure such as a building as a complex structure in which one part caused damage to another, but there may be liability where a distinct item (e.g. a boiler) causes damage to the rest of the structure.
- Comment:
  This is a very important case. It expressly overrules the decision in Anns v Merton LBC [1978] 5 BLR 1 and any subsequent cases decided 'in reliance on Anns'. It takes further the principles set out in L. & F. Estates Ltd v Church Commissioners [1988] 41 BLR 1 and effectively marks the end of actions in tort for the recovery of economic loss (except in the case of negligent misstatement). The courts are laying increasing stress upon contracts and third party purchasers and tenants are finding themselves without adequate remedy for defects against consultants and builders. Hence the growth in demands for assignable collateral warranties to create contractual relationships where none would otherwise exist.

3

GREAVES & CO. (CONTRACTORS) LTD v BAYNHAM MEIKLE & PARTNERS [1974] 3 All ER 666

- The Facts:
  The plaintiffs were builders who engaged the defendants as consultant engineers to design the structure of a warehouse required for the storing of full drums of oil which would be moved about on fork-lift stacker trucks. The design was executed in accordance with the relevant building regulations and codes of practice, the particularly relevant code of which contained a warning against structural damage which may be caused by vibrations set up by dynamic loads. The warehouse developed cracks, and the builders, who became liable to the owners, sought an indemnity from the defendant engineers. Expert evidence showed that the cracking was caused by random vibrations set up by the loaded trucks, of which the defendants had not taken sufficient account, having interpreted the code warning as referring only to repeated rhythmic impulses. Furthermore, a large number of professionals would have similarly interpreted the warning.
- Held:
  Because the defendants ought to have been aware that the floor of the warehouse would carry heavily laden trucks, and since they had been warned of the dangers of vibration generally, the law imposed a higher duty on them than it did on professionals normally. It was their duty to ensure that the floor was fit for its intended purpose, and they were in breach of that duty.
- Comment:
  The importance of this case lies in the fact that not only does a designer owe a general duty of care to the employer, but that contracts of this nature imply a term that the product should be fit for the purpose for which it is required. Care should therefore be taken to ensure that all available information as to proposed use is obtained prior to design.

4

SUTCLIFFE v THACKRAH & OTHERS [1974] 1 All ER 859

- The Facts:
  The defendant architects were employed by the plaintiff to design a house. There was no formal contract, but the defendants knew that the JCT Standard Form of Contract was to be used. Under clause 30 of the 1963 Edition of the Standard Form, the architect was empowered to issue interim certificates at specified intervals. Subsequently the builders became insolvent and, finding the work to be defective, the plaintiff brought an action against the architects, alleging supervisory negligence, and negligence in issuing two interim certificates. The defendants claimed that they were acting in an arbitral capacity and, provided that they acted honestly, they were under no duty to exercise care or professional skill. The Court of Appeal agreed with them, but the plaintiff appealed to the House of Lords.

- Held:
  An architect or valuer was generally liable to the employer if loss resulted from their negligence. However, immunity existed if the architect or valuer could show that, by agreement, they were appointed to act as an arbitrator or quasi-arbitrator to settle a specific dispute, and there was an agreement that their decision would be binding. The defendants had no immunity because
  (1) Issuing the interim certificate was not a decision resulting from a dispute.
  (2) There was no agreement that the architect's decision would be binding in respect of the value of the work.
  (3) The defedants owed the plaintiff a duty to exercise care and skill in issuing certificates.

- Comment:
  This case clearly denies the architect's immunity in respect of certification under the JCT Form of Contract. Even if the architect's powers were derived from some other form of contract, no immunity would exist unless the three major points of the judgment were satisfied. Architects should now exercise extreme care before issuing any certificate.

5

PACIFIC ASSOCIATES INC & ANO v BAXTER & OTHERS [1988] 44 BLR 33

- The Facts:
  The plaintiff entered into a contract with the employer to carry out dredging work in the Persian Gulf. The contract was on FIDIC Standard Form (1969 Edition). The plaintiff claimed that unexpected hard materials had been encountered, involving additional expense. The engineer refused to certify the claim for payment and the plaintiff started arbitration proceedings against the employer. The arbitration was settled and the plaintiff started proceedings on the same basis against the engineer alleging breach of a duty to use due care and to act impartially in certifying the payments which the plaintiff claimed as due in arbitration. The claim was rejected in the Official Referees Court and the plaintiff appealed.

- Held
  - The engineer's obligations to use skill and care were owed contractually to the employer.
  - The engineer did not assume liability to the contractor for economic loss arising out of breach of obligations in the FIDIC contract.
  - There was no basis on which the engineer could be said to owe the contractor a duty of care.
  - The engineer had a duty to the employer to act in accordance with the FIDIC contract. If the contractor wishes to challenge the engineer's performance, it should be done through the arbitration clause. There was no justification for imposing an additional liability in tort.

- Comment:
  This case indicates that the courts are unwilling to open up a *tortious* route where a plaintiff has a remedy in contract for damages. It can only be good news for the architect, but the courts are still some way from returning to the position in Bagot v Stevens Scanlon & Co [1964] 3 All ER 577 that professional people owed duties only in contract. The principles in Pacific Associates have been followed in the Canadian case of Edgeworth Construction Ltd v N. D. Lea & Associates Ltd [1991] 7 Const LJ 238. If the main contract, unusually, has no arbitration (or adjudication) clause or the employer becomes insolvent, the position is less clear.

6

SMITH v ERIC S. BUSH and HARRIS v WYRE FOREST DISTRICT COUNCIL [1989] 2 ER 514

- The Facts:
  In the Smith case, the plaintiff applied for a mortgage. The building society instructed the defendants who were surveyors and valuers to value the property and note anything likely to affect its value. They failed to notice a defective chimney and gave a favourable report. The plaintiff bought the house relying solely on the report, although she had been advised to get independent advice and the report contained a comprehensive disclaimer of liability. The chimney collapsed and the plaintiff claimed damages from the defendants in negligence. In the Harris case, the plaintiffs applied to the local Council for a loan for house purchase. The application form contained a disclaimer making clear that the valuation report was intended solely for the benefit of the Council which accepted no responsibility for the value or condition of the house. The Council advised the plaintiffs to obtain their own independent survey. They did not do so, but relied on the fact that they were offered a mortgage as indicative of the absence of serious faults. They proceeded with the purchase, but when they attempted to sell the house, serious faults became apparent and they brought an action in negligence against the Council and its agent. Both plaintiffs were successful at the first trial, but the Court of Appeal produced quite different results. An appeal was made to the House of Lords which considered both cases together.

- Held:
  The valuer was liable in both cases. He knew that 90% of purchasers relied on the valuation and did not obtain independent reports. At common law a party was free to exclude liability for negligence, but the Unfair Contract Terms Act 1977 must be considered. Section 11(3) provided that regard should be had to all 'circumstances obtaining when the liability arose or (but for the notice) was arisen' in deciding whether it would be fair and reasonable to allow reliance on a notice. The exclusion notices must satisfy the reasonableness test.
  In determining reasonableness the following questions should always be asked:
  - Did the parties have equal bargaining power?
  - Would it have been reasonably practicable for the purchaser to have obtained advice from another source?
  - How difficult was the survey?
  - What were the practical consequences?

(*Continued from page 6*)

Each case concerned a modest house and valuers knew the purchasers relied on their skill and care. In other situations, where large sums were at stake, the purchasers might be expected to commission independent surveys and the valuers might be considered to have acted reasonably in excluding or limiting their liability.

- Comment:
A milestone in the considerable caselaw on building surveys. The principles of liability are here relatively easily established on the basis of Hedley Byrne & Co Ltd v Heller & Partners Ltd [1963]. The interest is in the exclusion clauses. It used to be standard practice to include a comprehensive disclaimer clause whenever a building survey was undertaken, because they were often carried out for relatively small fees in a short period of time and there is a substantial risk of overlooking a major defect in such instances. This case not only affects any architect who undertakes a building survey, but extends to all cases where a professional person gives any kind of service and attempts to modify liability by inserting an exclusion clause. It is clear that such attempted exclusions will be examined with great care by the courts in the light of the Unfair Contract Terms Act. Attempted total exclusions of liability will rarely, if ever, succeed.

7

STOVIN-BRADFORD v VOLPOINT PROPERTIES LTD & ANOTHER [171] 3 All ER 570

- The Facts:
The plaintiff, an architect, designed and produced plans for the defendant company's proposed warehouses, and submitted the plans for planning permission which was subsequently granted. The architect had heard adverse reports of the defendant's dealings with architects, and when submitting his account for the work (the fees for which were considerably below RIBA scale) he expressly reserved his copyright of the design which was very distinctive, in that it included an unusual and pleasing diamond-shaped feature. The architect then withdrew from the project, but was later surprised to notice that the defendant company were building the warehouses to a design which incorporated the diamond-shaped feature.
- Held:
The defendants were liable for infringment of the plaintiff's copyright because the fee charged by the plaintiff was nominal, and did not carry an implied licence to use the plans produced, or the design concepts. Damages were assessed on the basis of what would be a fair fee for a licence to use the copyright in the plans for the purpose for which it was used.
- Comment:
This case suggests that, provided RIBA recommended fees are charged, the architect grants an implied licence to use the design. However, Lord Justice Salmon, one of the three judges hearing the appeal stated:

> I am by no means convinced that even if an architect were to charge the full scale fee for preparing drawings for planning permission purposes, in every case a licence to use the drawings would necessarily be implied.

The position was left uncertain. Now that the RIBA Scale is no longer mandatory, the question could become complicated unless the Standard Form of Agreement for the Appointment of an Architect (see page 27) is used, which makes specific provisions with regard to copyright. The Copyright Designs and Patents Act 1988 is also relevant.

8

JOHN BARKER CONSTRUCTION LTD v LONDON PORTMAN HOTEL LTD [1996] 83 BLR 31

- The Facts:
The claimants were builders who entered into a contract on JCT 80 terms to carry out refurbishment work to part of a hotel. There was a sectional completion supplement. Delays occurred, and the defendants entered into an acceleration agreement with the claimants. New completion dates were set, but further delays occurred and the claimants said they were entitled to an extension of time until practical completion. The architect gave only a partial extension and the claimants issued proceedings accordingly.
- Held:
The architect should have carried out a logical analysis of the impact of the delays on the claimant's planned programme and should not have made an impressionistic assessment. The extension should have borne a reasonable relationship to the delay. In making an extension of time, the architect should have had regard to the relevant events, not to the performance of the builders. Although the architect's decision was not made in bad faith, it was not properly based on an appreciation of the contract provisions.
- Comment:
The importance of this case lies in the emphasis placed by the court of the logical calculation of extensions of time. The claimant's case was supported by a computer programme and the judge viewed this with approval. Architects have traditionally treated their duty to 'estimate' a fair and reasonable extension of time as a permit to do little more than guess what might be a suitable period. Often, the estimate seems to have been based upon the amount by which the contract period was exceeded less the amount of delay that architects considered the builder had caused. This is, of course, the reverse of what architects should do. They should concentrate on the effect of relevant events on the contract completion date.

9

RUXLEY ELECTRONICS AND CONSTRUCTION LTD v
FORSYTH [1995] 73 BLR 1

- The Facts:
  The case concerned the construction of a swimming pool
  for Mr Forsyth. The pool turned out to be 9 inches
  shallower at the deepest part than was specified. The
  question was whether Mr Forsyth was entitled to have the
  pool entirely rebuilt in order to achieve the desired depth,
  even though it was agreed that the shallower depth was
  perfectly serviceable for all practical purposes, or whether he
  was merely entitled to receive some relatively modest sum in
  compensation.

- Held:
  Under a building contract, the appropriate measure of
  damages for defects is not the cost of reinstatement if the
  cost is out of all proportion to the benefit obtained. The
  alternative measure of damages, diminution in value, may
  result in a nominal sum.

- Comment:
  This case has clear implications for the construction
  industry. The employer is entitled to the building as
  specified in the contract documents. If some of the work is
  found to be defective, it is nothing more or less than a
  breach of contract and the contractor is obliged to rectify it.
  Where rectification of the breach will involve a great deal of
  expense and the benefit will be minimal, a contractor may
  be able to get away with a payment of modest
  compensation instead. It will not, of course, change the
  position, however expensive, if the employer will receive a
  measurable benefit from complete rectification or where the
  rectification is wholly concerned with defective work. For
  example, if a contractor builds a gable wall totally out of
  square so that a householder will be condemned to suffer
  something which will look bad and which will always
  necessitate angled cutting of carpets and fitted furniture,
  there is little doubt that the contractor will be obliged to
  rebuild or fund the cost of doing so. On the other hand, if
  the defect is simply that the contractor put in the wrong
  damp proof course, but it is working perfectly well and there
  is no reason why it should not continue to do so, it is
  unlikely that the contractor could be compelled to underpin
  the building to insert the correct material, although some
  compensation may have to be paid.

1 Housing Grants, Regeneration and Construction Act 1996

Part II, which specifically concerns 'Construction Contracts',
came into force on 1 May 1998. It gives statutory force to the
Scheme for Construction Contracts (England and Wales)
Regulations 1998 ('the Scheme'), the provisions of which
have effect as implied terms of all Constructions Contracts
covered by the Act if the parties do not incorporate terms of
similar effect into their contract.

Part II comprises 14 sections, i.e. s.104 to s.117 inclusive.

Sections 104 to 107 deal with the definitions and scope of
the terms used elsewhere throughout the remaining provisions.
Adjudication is dealt with under s.108 whilst s.109 to s.115
inclusive deal in varying contexts with the issue of payment.
Sections 116 to 117 are procedural.

The Act affects virtually all those engaged in the industry.

Most standard forms of contract have been amended to
comply with the requirements of the Act.

Construction contract

The Act defines a 'Construction Contract' in s.104. It includes:
- carrying out construction operations;
- arranging for carrying out construction operations by
  others;
- providing labour for carrying out construction
  operations;
- agreement to do architectural, design or surveying
  work;
- providing advice on building, engineering, interior or
  exterior decoration or landscape layout.

Construction operations

'Construction operations' is defined in s.105 as construction,
alteration, repair, etc. of buildings, structures, roadworks,
docks and harbours, powerlines, sewers, etc. It also includes
installation of fittings such as heating, electrical or air
conditioning, external or internal cleaning carried out as part
of construction and site clearance, tunnelling, foundations and
other preparatory work and painting or decorating.

Excluded are: drilling for natural gas, mineral extraction,
manufacture of certain components, construction or demolition
of plant where the primary activity is nuclear processing, effluent
treatment or chemicals, construction of artistic works, sign
writing and other peripheral installations (s.105(2)).

It does not apply where one of the parties intends to occupy
the subject of the construction operations (s.106) if residential
property.

Agreements in writing

The provisions apply only to 'agreements in writing' (s.107).
Apart from the obvious, they also cover situations where there
is no signature, where the parties agree orally by reference to
terms which are in writing and where an agreement is alleged
in arbitration by one party and not denied by the other.

Every construction contract must have specific clauses as follows:

Adjudication

Every construction contract must provide that either party will
have the right to refer any dispute(s) to 'adjudication' with the
object of obtaining a decision within 28 days of referral
(s.108). A party may give notice of intention to refer a dispute
to adjudication to the other, at any time, and the referral must
take place within 7 days. The adjudicator is required to reach
a decision within 28 days, but the parties may extend this
deadline by agreement. The adjudicator may extend the 28
days by up to a further 14 days if the referring party agrees.

The adjudicator may take the initiative in ascertaining the
facts and the law.

The adjudicator's decision is binding until the dispute is
determined by litigation, arbitration or by agreement. The parties
may agree to accept the adjudicator's decision as final.

All construction contracts must provide that the adjudicator
is not liable for acts or omissions except where there is bad faith.

Stage payments

The contractor will be entitled to 'stage payments' unless the
project duration is less than 45 days. The parties are free to
agree the intervals between payments and the amounts of
such payments.

Date for payment

Every contract must have the means of working out the amount due and the date on which it is due and must provide a final date for payment.

Set-off

Payment may not be withheld, nor money set-off unless notice has been given particularising the amount to be withheld and the grounds for withholding it. The notice must be given no later than the agreed period before final payment.

Suspension of work

If a sum has not been paid by the final date for payment and no effective notice withholding payment has been given, the contractor has the right, after 7 days' notice, to suspend work until payment is made.

Pay when paid

Except in cases of insolvency, a clause making payment to the contractor dependent upon receipt of payment from a third party is void. This is intended to outlaw the so-called pay-when-paid clause, but it may not be sufficient to do so. It does not take effect if the third party in question is insolvent.

2 Construction (Design and Management) Regulations 1994

These are regulations which place duties on clients, agents, designers and contractors to take account of health and safety, to co-ordinate and manage it effectively during all the stages of a project from inception to eventual repair and maintenance procedures.

They came into force on 31 March 1995 throughout the UK and in certain circumstances elsewhere (reg. 20). In Northern Ireland, the Regulations are dated 1995.

They are administered by the Health and Safety Executive under the Health and Safety at Work Act 1974.

The key parts of the Regulations:

- Clients and agents must be reasonably satisfied that they are using competent persons for key roles and that sufficient resources are earmarked.

- A planning supervisor must be appointed to co-ordinate health and safety aspects at the design stage.
- The planning supervisor is responsible for the health and safety plan and health and safety file preparation.
- The designer must perform duties in order to avoid, reduce or control risks during construction and maintenance.
- The principal contractor must develop the health and safety plan and ensure compliance by all on site.
- Other contractors on the project must cooperate with the principle contractor.
- On completion, a health and safety file is produced which serves as a maintenance manual, but also warns of particular risks and dangers.
- Domestic householders do not have duties under the Regulations.

The Health and Safety Executive have produced an 'Approved Code of Practice' referring to the Regulations. The Code has a special status. If persons are prosecuted for breach of health and safety law and it is proved that they have failed to comply with the Code, they will be found to be at fault by a court unless they are able to show that they have complied with the law in some other way.

3 Contracts (Rights of Third Parties) Act 1999

This came into force on 11 May 2000 and applies throughout the UK. It gives entitlement to third parties, who are not parties to the contract, to enforce certain rights, but not unless:

- the contract gives the third party a right;
- the terms confer a benefit (unless it is clear that a benefit was not intended to be conferred);
- the third party is identified in the contract: by name, class or description.

The right may only be enforced in accordance with the terms of the contract, and the party against whom the third party seeks to enforce the terms may use any defences and remedies available under the contract and may raise any set-off or counterclaim. In some instances, the third party may be treated as a party to an arbitration agreement in the contract.

Parties to a contract may expressly exclude third party rights under that contract. This is now the usual approach.

The need for safeguards

The law can be seen as a complex web of rules and procedures that either control or affect the actions of an individual or group. Transgression of the rules, whether intentional or otherwise, might lead to the implementation of prescribed punitive or compensatory measures by the controlling authorities.

In the field of construction, the potential problems arising from the intricacy of relationships and tasks, coupled with the ever-changing circumstances and conditions within which they are set, have led to the implementation of a number of precautions and remedies to either prevent or allow for certain contingencies. The most important of these are:

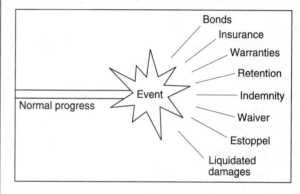

Bonds

Performance bonds fulfil a similar role to insurance where, for example, they may enable the employer to claim compensation from the underwriting surety in the event of non-completion by the contractor.

The Standard Form has optional bonds to offer security should advance payments or payment for materials off-site be made by the Employer.

Insurance (see page 11)

Contracts of insurance may be entered into by the architect, the contractor, the sub-contractor and the employer to protect their respective interests. In the case of the contractor, this is a contractual obligation under the Standard Form clause 21.

Safeguards and Remedies

Warranties (see page 68)

These are legally enforceable assurances given by parties in respect of their goods and services. They are contracts which run alongside and are collateral to another contract. They are often referred to as 'collateral contracts'. It is now usual for architects and other professionals to be asked for warranties (sometimes called 'duty of care agreements') as a result of the difficulty in bringing actions in tort against architects following D. & F. Estates v Church Commissioners [1988] and Murphy v Brentwood District Council [1990]. The warranties may be required in favour of the client, future tenants of the property, future purchasers or funding institutions. Model forms of warranty have been jointly developed by the British Property Federation, the Royal Institute of British Architects, the Royal Institution of Chartered Surveyors and the Association of Consulting Engineers. Use of these forms is not mandatory and a wide range of specifically drafted warranties may be presented to the architect for signature. Some of the topics included in such warranties include:

- standard of care
- consequential losses
- indemnity
- deleterious materials
- professional indemnity
- surrender of copyright
- assignment without consent
- extension of limitation period
- novation

See David Cornes and Richard Winward, *Winward Fearon on Collateral Warranties*, 2nd Edn, 2002, Blackwell Publishing, Oxford.

See page 9 for the Contracts (Rights of Third Parties) Act 1999.

Retention

At each stage of payment, an agreed percentage (which may vary from 3% on medium to large projects to 5% on small projects) will be retained by the employer. Half of this may be released upon the issuance of a Certificate of Practical Completion. Payment of the balance may depend upon the Completion of Making Good Defects or it may be retained until the Final Certificate, depending upon the form of contract in use. Recent caselaw has established that where the retention money is stated to be a trust fund (i.e. under JCT 98) the employer has an obligation to place it in a separate bank account even where the parties have deleted that stipulation from the contract.

Indemnity

An indemnity (or guarantee) is given by one party to secure another against loss or damage from specific liabilities (for example, Standard Form clause 20).

Waiver

A waiver indicates the relinquishing of specific rights by a party.

Estoppel

This is a doctrine which exists to prevent one party behaving inconsistently with his or her representation to another, in reliance of which the other has acted and suffered loss. In these circumstances, the first party could be 'estopped' from taking advantage of the situation by the courts.

Liquidated damages

These are damages which are agreed between the employer and the contractor (and stated in the Appendix). They provide a settled method of assessing damages arising out of late completion (that is, £x per day or per week beyond the Date for Completion). The employer does not have to prove loss before deducting the damages and is entitled to deduct the amount stated (but no more) whether the loss is greater or less than the amount or even if the employer gains as a result of the delay. The amount stated must be a genuine pre-estimate by the employer of the loss honestly believed to be incurred. The contractor may avoid paying liquidated damages:

- by obtaining an extension of time;
- by showing that the Date for Completion no longer applies because the architect has failed to give an extension of time when one was due;
- by showing that the amount stated in the Appendix is legally a penalty (e.g. it is much greater than could possibly represent a realistic pre-estimate of the likely amount).

Claims: settle or defend

If a complaint is made on the basis that legal obligations have not been fulfilled, the party so charged may admit responsibility and settle the claim by agreed damages, or other suitable means of compensation. Alternatively, the charge may be refuted, in which case it is likely that the conflict will be dealt with by adjudication, arbitration or litigation through the civil courts.

Shared liability

It is possible in tort that parties may share the responsibility, in which case, they become JOINT TORTFEASORS in the same action. Joint tortfeasors are jointly and severally liable.

Time limits

Lapse of time may afford protection to a negligent party. The Limitation Act 1980 sets down time limits in respect of certain types of action, notably:

- 6 years in respect of a contract under hand (i.e. a simple contract)
- 12 years in respect of a contract entered into as a deed.

Beyond these periods, if an action is commenced, the defendant or respondent could defend it on the basis that is was not brought within the relevant limitation period. This would be the case even if they were liable as claimed.

The Latent Damage Act 1986 lays down time limits in respect of negligent actions involving property. They are either:

- 6 years from the day the cause of the action arose

or

- 3 years from the date the plaintiff acquired knowledge of the damage and the identity of the defendant, if this period expires later than the six years noted above.

In any case, a longstop period of 15 years from the date of the negligent action applies, after which no action can be brought.

References

LAW, pp. 113, 162, 190.
ARCHITECT'S LEGAL HANDBOOK, pp. 172–7.

A contract of insurance arises when one party undertakes to make payments for the benefit of another in the event of certain events taking place (an insurance contract). The conditions upon which such a payment would occur are usually described in detail in the Policy.

The consideration (see page 51) necessary to validate the contract is called the premium, and insurance cover is often secured through a broker. Many architects utilise the services offered by:

RIBA Insurance Agency
133 Houndsditch
London
EC3A 7AH

Types

There are two kinds of insurance:
- INDEMNITY INSURANCE.
  This ensures the payment of compensation for losses incurred by certain events, e.g. fire, motor safety or third party liability.
- NON-INDEMNITY INSURANCE.
  In this case a specific sum is paid on the occurrence of a specified event, e.g. attainment of a certain age.

Contracts of insurance are said to be 'of the utmost good faith' (*uberrimae fidei*). This means that all material facts must be disclosed to insurers which might affect their willingness to accept the risk. Failure to disclose may render the contract voidable. Indemnity insurance should be considered in three categories:

PROFESSIONAL INDEMNITY
SITE INSURANCE
LATENT DEFECTS INSURANCE

Professional indemnity

Professional indemnity insurance is a precautionary measure often taken to protect the architect, any partners, and employees from claims arising from their negligent acts. Care should be taken to ensure that each new partner or employee is covered under the terms of the policy, and that any unusual features of the office (involvement in overseas work, for example) are covered.

Coverage

Coverage of indemnity insurance may include:
- professional negligence
- infringement of copyright
- loss of documents
- recovery of professional fees
- dishonesty of employees
- defamation

Continuing coverage (run-off insurance) on withdrawal or retirement by a member should be carefully considered in the light of recent caselaw.

Site insurance

The contractor is responsible for taking control of the site, and must maintain insurances to cover liability (and that of sub-contractors) in respect of personal injury (JCT Standard Form of Contract 1998, clause 21.1.1.1). Contractors must also insure against damage to the property arising from their actions.

The architect has the right (clause 21.1.2) to inspect the contractor's insurance in respect of the site, and should the latter default, the employer may insure and deduct the cost of the premium from the contractor's fees.

The site must also be insured against damage by fire and other accidents in the joint names of the employer and contractor.

Adjustments to the site insurance should be made:
- on sectional completion, if appropriate;
- on practical completion;
- in the event of any material change that may affect the policy.

Latent defects insurance

This is sometimes known as BUILD (Building Users Insurance Against Latent Defects). It is a non-cancellable insurance against major latent defects for a fixed period (usually 10 years) involving payment of a single premium by the building owner and it is assignable to future owners of the building.

Further coverage

It is also advisable to consider the need of insuring against:
- EMPLOYER'S LIABILITY, covering the death or injury of employees under the Employees Liability (Compulsory Insurance) Act 1969;
- PUBLIC LIABILITY, to cover third parties;
- BUILDING AND CONTENTS, either on an indemnity or reinstatement basis;
- MOTOR CARS, if used for business purposes.

It may also be worthwhile considering insurance in respect of:
TRAVEL HAZARDS
STAFF WELFARE
PENSIONS

Points to remember

- Keep all policies safely at the principal place of business.
- Notify insurers of all matters which may affect the risk ('good faith' principle).
- Ensure that renewal dates are noted in order that premiums can be promptly paid.
- Check all policies periodically to ensure that the amount of cover is adequate.
- Consider the benefit of index-linked policies.
- Notify insurers of all new staff relevant to the Professional Indemnity policy.
- Never take insurance cover for granted. If in doubt as to whether a risk is covered, check with the insurers first.

References

ARCHITECT'S HANDBOOK OF PRACITCE MANAGEMENT, pp. 56–7, 79–81.
THE ARCHITECT'S GUIDE TO RUNNING A JOB, pp. 76–7.
ARCHITECT'S LEGAL HANDBOOK, pp. 94–103, 341–3.

MEMO

To :
From : Tom
Date : Bill
Concerning : 4th Jan
: Unpaid fees

Tom — have been looking through outstanding a/cs & note that your Mr Fox hasn't settled the final account we sent to him 6 months ago. Please could you deal with this ASAP.

LOCKE, STOCKE and BARRELL

A.Locke.LLB(Lond).
J.Stocke.MA(Oxon).   SOLICITORS
B.Barrell.BA(Rangoon).

Our Ref: AL/gy
Your Ref: 1, Fore Hall
                                                 Cringing,
                                                 Wilts.

                                                 15.1.02

Dear Sirs,

WITHOUT PREJUDICE

re: A.Payne Esq.

We have been consulted by your above-named ex-employee who informs us that he suffered an injury while preparing drawings in the course of his employment.

We understand that Mr Payne fell from a faulty chair and damaged the third finger of his right hand, getting it caught in the computer keyboard. In consequence, Mr Payne lost much of the sensitivity in this finger and, being a keen bowls enthusiast is now deprived of his major pastime.

We have advised our client that he has a good case in tort, since the accident resulted from your firm's negligence. However, our client is disposed to settle this matter for a payment of £900.

We look forward to receiving your comments,

Yours faithfully,

Locke Stocke & Barrell

Locke, Stocke and Barrell

Fair and Square,
ellovet,

JUSTIN CASE

Insurance
Broker   4 JAN.02

Dear Sirs,   re: Policy No.163468-Fire Insurance

I note from our records that the premium in respect of your above-numbered policy is due on the 14th of this month. I would draw your attention to the availability of index-linked policies, which lessen the need to constantly reassess the amount of cover necessary. If you would be interested in discussing a transfer to this type of policy, please telephone me to arrange an appointment.

Yours faithfully,

J. Case

J.Case

Tative Approach, Cringing, Wilts

DESK DIARY

JAN 21

Re: Fox, outstanding Fees.
Check today to see if he pays up, following our letter.
If not, discuss with Bill whether or not to sue.
Is it worth it for this amount? The costs involved may
not make it worthwhile. Might consider another letter
From solicitors or a small claims action though.

JAN 22

Re: Payne's Finger.
- Have acknowledged receipt of letter from L.S.B,
but haven't commented.
- Have informed our solicitors & insurers -
sounds like a try-on, but you never know -
I didn't know Arthur played bowls!

Fair and Square

CHARTERED ARCHITECTS

B.FAIR.dip.arch.RIBA.
T.SQUARE.B.Arch.RIBA.AFAS.

Our Ref: TS/vn

4, The Hellovet
Cringing,
Wilts.

Dear Mr Fox,

Jan.7th.02

**re: Outstanding fees for house extension at
Witt's End**

Further to our letters of the 23rd Sept. and the 3rd Dec. 2001,
we note that your final account is still outstanding to the
sum of £780.

We regret to inform you that if payment in full is not
received within 14 days of the date of this letter, we shall
be compelled to institute proceedings against you in the
County Court.

We look forward to hearing from you,

Yours sincerely,

Fair & Square

Fair and Square

A.Fox Esq.
Taxfrey Haven,
Cringing,
Wilts.

MEMO

To   : Tom
From   : Bill
Date.   : 7th Jan
Concerning   : Insurance renewal

Do we need to increase cover re
increased property value & new
office equipment? If so, by how much?
Motor premiums also due soon — we
must insure RoyTing's Mini, as he's
using it for site visits, and may not
be covered on his domestic policy.
Broker suggests index-linked
policies — sounds good.

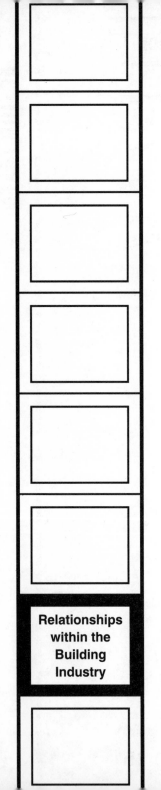

THE BUILDING INDUSTRY

Contents

Relationships within the Building Industry

Parties operating within the construction industry have different legal personalities according to the type of association to which they belong. This personality affects the relationship between the law, the employer and the individual. Major methods of operating a business are:

1. Single individual

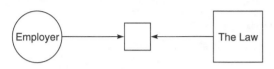

This is the simplest form of association, where the responsibilities and liabilities are clearly defined, e.g. a sole practitioner of architecture or a builder.

2. Partnership

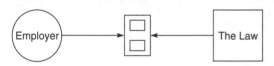

A partnership exists where two or more individuals carry on a business in common with a view to profit, the profit to be shared in the proportions agreed by the partners. In general, partnership is governed by the provisions of the Partnership Act 1890, and it is a common method of practising architecture as it enables the parties to share their expertise, capital and resources.

The formation of a partnership does not limit the responsibility of the individuals involved, and partners remain personally liable for all negligent acts of the firm. However, the partnership may sue or be sued in the name of the partnership.

Formation

The partnership relationship can be created by:
- conduct of the parties;
- oral agreement;
- written agreement.

The latter is by far the most satisfactory, where all terms, conditions and implications of the relationship can be fully explored before a binding agreement is made.

Types of practitioner

a   THE EQUITY PARTNER

This is a full partnership arrangement, where the partner enjoys the full benefits and responsibilities of the firm.

b   THE SALARIED PARTNER

A salaried partnership is in effect a 'name only' arrangement, enabling recipients to have their names on the letterhead of the firm. However, the implication may be that they share the same liabilities as the equity partners, and an indemnity should be obtained from the equity partners in respect of partnership liabilities and debts. Before accepting a salaried partnership, it should be remembered that all rights of redundancy pay and unfair dismissal compensation would be lost, and that the income tax position may also be affected. However, a salaried partnership may have advantages in the form of a share of the profits or as an interim step before final commitment to the firm.

c   THE LIMITED PARTNER

The Limited Partnership Act 1907 provides for this type of partner, whose liability is limited to the extent of an individual's capital investment. Such a partner does not usually become involved in the management of the firm.

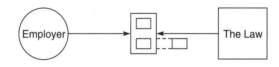

d   THE ASSOCIATE

Although a salaried position, an associateship indicates a certain status, and may carry a small share in the firm's profits. There can be uncertainty as to the liability of the position in relation to the partners, and, as with salaried partners, the extent of the responsibilities and liabilities of the associate should be clearly stated in the agreement or letter of acceptance. The position should also be made clear in the associate's dealings with the public so as to avoid the possible assumption of equality with the partners (for example, letterheads should be clearly marked with the associate's name and position, preferably distinct from those of the partners).

e   THE DIRECTOR

The architect can carry on business as a director of a limited company (see page 16), subject to professional indemnity insurance provisions.

Termination

The partnership agreement can be terminated by:
- expiration of an agreed time period;
- completion of a designated task or project;
- death of one of the partners;
- bankruptcy of a partner;
- retirement of a partner;
- mutual agreement;
- by order of the court;
- by subsequent illegality.

In some cases, it is desirable to include provisions in the partnership agreement to enable the firm to continue despite certain of the above events happening, e.g. death.

Title and tax

a   Since the Companies Act 1981, it is unnecessary to register the firm name and the names of all the partners, but if the word 'architect' is used in the firm name, ARB's approval is needed.

b   Partners are liable to income tax under Schedule D, but not to corporation tax. However, they should ensure that a tax reserve is maintained to satisfy their annual obligations.

Limited Liability Partnership

This is governed by the Limited Liability Partnerships Act 2000 and intended to combine the best features of partnership and limited companies. Key features:
- A Limited Liability Partnership (LLP) will be a separate legal entity from its members.
- No joint and several liability.
- 'Designated Members' act in a similar way to a company secretary.
- Audited accounts must be filed.

It combines the organisational flexibility and tax status of a partnership with limited liability for its members.

3. Limited companies

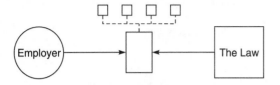

A limited company is a form of corporation limited in liability to the amount of shares or guarantee. It exists as a separate legal entity distinct from its shareholders, whose personal wealth is immune from claims made against the company. The assets of a limited company are contributed by its members, who buy shares representing the limit of their responsibility in the company.

Types

There are two kinds of limited company:
- PUBLIC LIMITED COMPANIES
  These have unlimited membership and have their shares quoted on the Stock Exchange. The shares are freely transferable.
- PRIVATE LIMITED COMPANIES
  These are usually smaller and, while there is no limitation on the number of members, if membership falls below two for six months, personal liability can be incurred. The shares are not freely transferable.

Formation

The formation of a limited company requires:
- Articles of Association
- Memorandum of Agreement

Articles regulate the management and procedures that the company will follow, while the Memorandum sets out the objectives of the company. (In the case of a public company, this is dealt with in the Charter or Statute which created it.) The powers of the company thus stated must not be exceeded, otherwise the company acts *ultra vires* (beyond its powers).

4. Unlimited companies

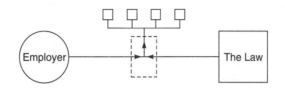

These are fairly unusual forms of corporations, as the shareholders do not have their liability limited to the value of their shares. Advantages of this form of association may include the achievement of corporate status and certain legal and tax benefits.

5. Group practice

This is a useful form of association often found in the practice of architecture, where the advantages may include:
- shared resources
- shared capital
- shared expertise and knowledge
- fluidity of staff allocation

There are five types of group practice:
1 THE GROUP ASSOCIATION
  This is a loose arrangement of architectural firms, pooling knowledge and experience but retaining their individual identities in their dealings with employers.
2 SHARED FACILITIES
  Several firms may share facilities and operate either singly or in unison.
3 GROUP CO-ORDINATING FIRM
  Here, elements of a master plan are delegated to separate firms. They are co-ordinated by the architect responsible for the initial production of the master plan, who also remains answerable to the employer.
4 SINGLE PROJECT GROUP PARTNERSHIP
  The partnership exists for a specified time, or for a specified purpose only, at the end of which it automatically dissolves.
5 GROUP PARTNERSHIP
  Where firms retain their individual identities, but combine together in a continuing relationship for certain projects.

Other forms

Other forms of association connected with parties involved in the construction industry include:
  TRADE UNIONS
  LOCAL AUTHORITIES
  THE CROWN
  PUBLIC CORPORATIONS

Trade unions

These are groups formed within the trades with the objective of collectively bargaining for pay and conditions of employment.

Local authorities

These are corporate bodies whose constitution and powers are derived from statutes. Their contractual powers are similar to those of an incorporated company, where the council is vicariously responsible for its employees. (Professional employees, however, may have a personal liability in tort regardless of this relationship.)

The authorities are composed of metropolitan, county and district councils, each consisting of elected councillors.

The Crown

This title refers to all governmental powers expressed through the Civil Service at central government level. (It also refers to the rights and immunities of the reigning monarch.) Since 1947, a government department may be sued through the ordinary courts.

Public corporations

These are concerned with the nationalised industries, and were created by statute to be operated by the State. Their contractual powers are essentially the same as incorporated companies (that is, they may not operate *ultra vires*).

References

LAW, pp. 87–93.
ARCHITECT'S LEGAL HANDBOOK, pp. 309–20.
PM HANDBOOK, pp. 47–51.
THE ARCHITECT IN PRACTICE, pp. 51–65.
RIBA 'GUIDE TO GROUP PRACTICE & CONSORTIA'.

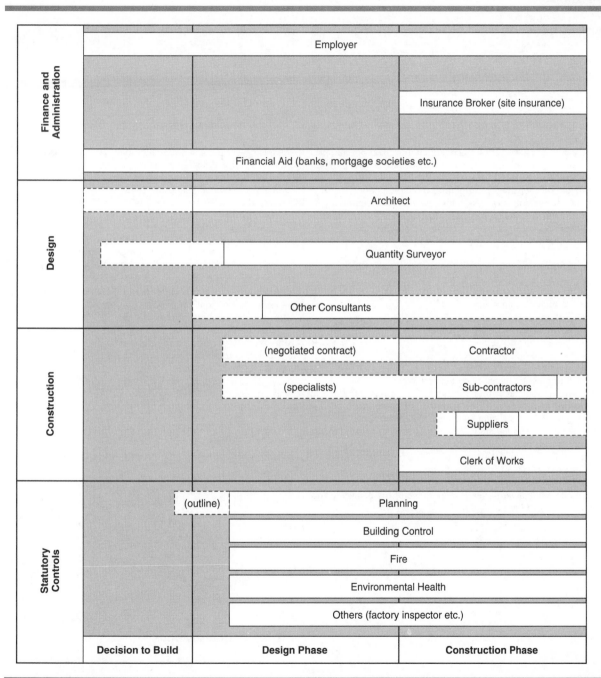

	Decision to Build	Design Phase	Construction Phase
Finance and Administration	Employer		
			Insurance Broker (site insurance)
	Financial Aid (banks, mortgage societies etc.)		
Design	Architect		
	Quantity Surveyor		
		Other Consultants	
Construction		(negotiated contract)	Contractor
		(specialists)	Sub-contractors
			Suppliers
			Clerk of Works
Statutory Controls	(outline)	Planning	
		Building Control	
		Fire	
		Environmental Health	
		Others (factory inspector etc.)	

Related organisations

Professional institutes and associations (trade, standards and research) within the building industry include:

Acoustics, Institute of
Advisory Conciliation and Arbitration Service
Agrément Board
Arbitrators, Chartered Institute of
Architectural Technologists, British Institute of
Architects, Association of Consultant
Architects and Surveyors Institute
Architects Registration Board
Architects, Royal Institute of British
Brick Development Association
Building Control Institute
Building, Chartered Institute of
Building Research Establishment
Building Services Engineers, Chartered Institute of
Building Services Research and Information Association
Cement Association, British
Chartered Surveyors, Royal Institution of
Civil Engineering Contractors Association
Civil Engineers, Institution of
Clerk of Works of Great Britain, Institute of
Construction Confederation
Construction Industry Research and Information Association
Designers, Chartered Society of
Electrical Engineers, Institution of
Facilities Management, British Institute of
Fire Officers Association
Fire Protection Association
Heating and Ventilation Contractors Association
House Building Council, National
Joint Contracts Tribunal
Landscape Institute
Master Builders, Federation of
Mechanical Engineers, Institution of
National Building Specification Services
Planning Supervisors, Association of
Plumbing, Institute of
Property Federation, British
Standards Institution, British
Steel Construction Institute
Structural Engineers, Institution of
Timber Research and Development Association
Town Planning Institute, Royal

Addresses of organisations which may be of most use to the architect are included on pages 100 and 101.

The Architect/Others

The architect/employer

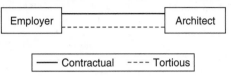

The relationship between the architect and employer is primarily contractual, and as such is governed by the terms of the contract between them. The contract invariably formalises a relationship of AGENCY, where the architect (the agent) acts as the employer's representative, working solely in the latter's best interests. Agency may be:

- UNIVERSAL, where for example, there is a power of attorney;
- GENERAL, within a defined area of duty (for example, a solicitor);
- SPECIAL, where the contract involved is for a specified purpose (such as the design and supervision of a construction project). This type of agency is nearly always detailed in a written agreement.

Agents are expected to work with the level of skill normally associated with their profession or occupation, and be concerned not to allow a conflict to arise between their own interests and those of their principal. The agency authority of the architect is limited to the terms of the appointment, and no authority is provided, for example, to vary the contract between the contractor and employer unless express powers are granted for such a purpose.

The architect's contract with the employer is one 'for services' rather than a contract 'of service'. This distinction depends on the degree of control exercised by the employer, and affects his or her vicarious liability in tort. The general rule holds an employer vicariously liable for acts of those employed under a contract of service (see page 30 for Employer Profile).

The architect/consultant

Where services necessary to a construction project are outside the normal services offered by the architect, specialists may be employed directly by the employer on advice from the architect. This separation of the roles of architect and consultant prevents any possibility of claims for vicarious responsibility between the two.

The following areas are outside normal architectural services:

- quantity surveying (see page 19)
- town planning
- civil engineering
- structural engineering
- mechanical engineering
- electrical engineering
- industrial design
- interior design
- landscape and garden design
- furniture design
- graphic design

More care must be taken when the architect wishes the employer to contract with a consultant for work within the architect's normal services, delegated due to time, staff shortages etc. In such circumstances, the consultant's responsibilities and liabilities should be carefully detailed in the agreement to avoid any confusion in the event of loss or damage. Furthermore, the hiring of such a consultant may justify a reduction in the architect's fee.

Whatever arrangements are eventually made, the employer should be made aware as early as possible of the necessity and implications of hiring consultants.

The architect/contractor

There is no contractual connection between these parties, as the contractor is directly responsible to the employer under the building contract. However, most contracts for construction contain provisions enabling the architect to fulfil certain prescribed duties in the capacity of agent (Standard Form clauses 2 and 4).

Errors made by the architect which cause loss to the contractor could not lead to an action in contract (see page 51), but could form the basis for a claim against the employer. This may in turn lead to an action by the employer against the architect for breach of the contract between them.

Alternatively, the contractor could sue the architect in tort, where no contractual connection is necessary but the chances of recovering damages are less certain.

A similar situation arises between the architect and the sub-contractors (whose contract will be with the contractor or employer), and the suppliers (who will deal directly with the contractors and sub-contractors).

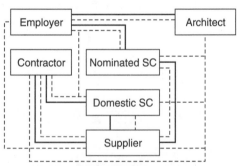

References

ARCHITECT'S HANDBOOK OF PRACTICE MANAGEMENT, pp. 209–13.
ARCHITECT'S LEGAL HANDBOOK, pp. 8–28.
THE ARCHITECT IN PRACTICE, pp. 81–101, 133–8.

Appointment

On most larger construction projects, a quantity surveyor would be instructed, essentially for the purpose of preparing estimates during the design stages, preparing bills of quantities and generally controlling cost throughout the building stages.

At what level of construction the employment of a quantity surveyor becomes viable depends on the nature of the work. Should the employer be reluctant to make an appointment, it may be necessary to point out that the work needed falls outside the normal architectural services and, if undertaken by the architect, will merit additional fees.

RICS

The Chartered Quantity Surveyor is a member of the Royal Institution of Chartered Surveyors, a respected professional body which comments on proposed legislation in the field of management, valuation and development of property, and planning provisions. It also aims to ensure high academic and professional standards in its members, and, among other things, it provides a useful cost information service for those involved in the construction industry.

The RICS is represented on the Joint Contracts Tribunal Ltd, and on most other British bodies associated with the construction industry.

The quantity surveyor might be described as a 'building economist', and as such plays an important part in the construction process.

Normal services

Normal services offered by the quantity surveyor include:
- cost advice on the proposed scheme;
- advice on the economics of the project, and preparation of a budget;

- given a fixed cost, advice on size and structure;
- advice on cost feasibility at the outline and scheme design stages;
- cost assessment of detailed design and production drawings against the cost plan;
- advice on tendering and type of contract suitable for the project;
- preparation of documents for arranging tenders and the building contract;
- preparation of bills of quantities;
- examination of tenders;
- ongoing check on the cost plan throughout the construction phase;
- valuations for interim certificates;
- preparation of the final account including adjustment of the contract sum for variations and claims for delay;
- advice on the financial implications of unplanned actions during construction (for example, variations).

Additional services

Additional services of the quantity surveyor might include:
- cost in use studies involving discounted cash flow techniques;
- valuation or reports (structural schedules of defects, etc.);
- advice on capital investment policy, and cost implications of site selection;
- advice on comparative costs of specialised building types and on performance specifications;
- life cycle cost analysis.

Preliminary advice

Even if a quantity surveyor is not appointed for a project, it may still be useful for the architect to consult one for general advice on approximate costs at the beginning of a scheme, at the sketch design stage. A quantity surveyor is able to judge the size and type of building feasible having regard to the finance available, and may thus save the architect a great deal of unnecessary work.

The employer usually contracts directly with the quantity surveyor, using the standard form produced by the Royal Institution of Chartered Surveyors for this purpose.

Other surveyors

Members of the Royal Institution of Chartered Surveyors practice in a number of fields other than quantity surveying:
- agricultural surveying
- auctioneering
- building surveying
- estate agency
- forestry management
- hydrographic surveying
- housing management
- land agency
- land economy
- land surveying
- town planning
- urban estate management
- valuation surveying
- mining surveying
- mineral surveying

In addition, THE CONTRACTOR'S SURVEYOR, whose role is more that of a building accountant than building economist, is a full-time employee of the contractor. Such an individual is often involved in submitting interim valuations, agreeing rates for variations, administration of sub-contracts, preparation of claim submissions and agreement of the final account.

References

ARCHITECT'S HANDBOOK OF PRACTICE MANAGEMENT, pp. 170, 193, 195, 201
THE ARCHITECT IN PRACTICE, pp. 4, 10, 201, 202, 224, 225.

1, Thewist Drive,
Cringing,
Wilts

February 11th.

Dear Mr Square,
        I am still not happy about the expense involved
in appointing a quantity surveyor as you suggested at our
last meeting. I always understood that such matters could be
dealt with by the architect. Unless you can assure me
otherwise, I would rather not be put to this added expense.

                                    Yours sincerely,

                                    B. Careful

B.Careful

MEMO

To   Tom

From   Bill

Date   15th Feb.

Concerning R.Tring — Associateship

Roy informs me that he's keen on our
proposal to make him an associate on
the terms mentioned, but he's rather
concerned about his position with
regard to his personal liability
Can we clarify the position for him?

Tom,
        We're a bit pushed for time
on the factory job — why
don't we push out the
tendering work to a consultant?
Could you suggest someone?

                                    Bill

DESK DIARY

FEB 18

Re: Roy's Associateship.
Must contact our insurers & inform them of the new position.

FEB 19

Fair and Square

CHARTERED ARCHITECTS

B.FAIR.dip.arch.RIBA.
T.SQUARE.B.Arch.RIBA.AFAS.

TS/vn

4, The Hellove
Cringing,
Wilts.

Dear Mr Careful,

12.2.02

re: Proposed development at Cheapsgate, Cringing

Thank you for your letter of the 11th Feb, expressing concern
in respect of appointing a quantity surveyor on the above
project. We appreciate your desire to keep costs at a minimum,
but are of the opinion that a quantity surveyor would make a
valuable contribution to the scheme for the following reasons:

1. A quantity surveyor specialises in building
economics, and is therefore able to provide you
with expert advice regarding structure, materials,
methods of construction etc. most appropriate and
economically viable for your particular project.
2. A quantity surveyor is also a building accountant,
and can not only plan and check costs before and
during the project, but will prepare Bills of
Quantities, periodical and final valuations and
advice on proposed or necessary variations that may
occur.
3. Although architects can deal with measurement and
valuation, work in this field falls outside the
Architect's Normal Services (as stated in your copy of
the Standard Form of Agreement for the Appointment of
an Architect), and extra fees for this work would become
chargeable under Schedule Two.

I hope the points raised in this letter adequately satisfy
your doubts, and we look forward to receiving your instructions
regarding the appointment of a quantity surveyor in due course.

Yours sincerely,

Fair & Square
Fair and Square

BILL - GOT YOUR MEMO ABOUT ROY'S ASSOCIATESHIP. SUGGEST THE FOLLOWING
POINTS SHOULD BE COVERED IN A LETTER OF CONFIRMATION TO KEEP
THE RECORDS STRAIGHT:

1 DETAILS OF SALARY
2 DETAILS OF PROFIT SHARING
3 CAREFUL DEFINITION OF RESPONSIBILITIES
  OF THE PARTNERSHIP (REMEMBER INSURANCES).
4 REQUIREMENT OF CONTINUING RIBA MEMBERSHIP
5 CLEAR DEFINITION OF THE ASSOCIATE STATUS
  ON LETTER-HEAD AND IN OUR BROCHURE

Tom.

MEMO

To : Bill
From : Tom
Date : 18th Feb.
Concerning : subbing out work. - Careful!

This phase is part of basic services - if someone else is
employed we have to reduce our fees. If we employ someone
ourselves, responsibilities/liabilities start getting complex.
Couldn't we ask Roy to take a look at it?

T.

THE ARCHITECT IN PRACTICE

Contents

**RIBA
Work Stage
A**

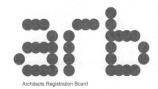

Architects Registration Board

The RIBA

The major professional organisation for architects was founded in 1834 and is located in Portland Place. Its objectives are:
- to promote the highest standards of architecture;
- to conserve and improve the architectural environment;
- to provide a single voice for the profession as a whole.

Membership

The RIBA has four classes of member:
- chartered
- graduate
- student
- subscriber

Chartered members may refer to themselves as 'chartered architect' and use the affix RIBA. In countries where registration is a legal requirement, the title and affix may be used only when the practising member is registered.

Membership in the chartered, graduate and student classes is secured by subscription and qualifications from, or study at, recognised institutions.

Membership in the subscriber class is secured by subscription.

Honorary Fellows and Honorary Corresponding Members are appointed by Council.

Structure

The Council of the RIBA is the governing body of the Institute and is headed by the president. It comprises the immediate past president, a past president, vice presidents and nationally and regionally elected members. The work of the Council is co-ordinated by a Board which is chaired by the president. The RIBA carries out a number of functions, which are grouped under a number of committees and task groups.

1 Practice Committee

Responsible for bringing members' knowledge and experience to bear on policy, priorities and professional issues within the field of practice including:
- Identification of strategic changes which are occurring and which should occur and giving appropriate advice on the implications for practice services provided by the RIBA departments and its companies.
- Advising on policy issues, including response to government on practice issues and advising on the wording of practice documents which require Council approval and the identification of key issues for study.
- Advising on and monitoring priorities, development and performance of practice services and identifying key issues for future policy formation and the provision of services.
- Overseeing liaison on practice matters between RIBA and related bodies, including CIC (and its members separately), JCT, ARB, BSI and BRE.
- Advising on practice policy and strategy.
- Reviewing implementation of Council policies and the progress of work against agreed objectives.
- Advising upon or judging as appropriate issues involving professional standards and practices and in other specialist areas where members have expertise.
- Appointment of task groups and specialist advisors for relevant projects.

2 Finance Committee

Responsible for:
- Institute's long- and short-term financial affairs.
- The budget.
- Financial business, investment and borrowing of funds.

It also provides accounting services for the RIBA subsidiary companies:
- RIBA Services Ltd/Library Planning Consultants Ltd. Handles technical and advisory services to the profession and the building industry; producing product data, office library services and developing the CI/Sfb system of classification.
- RIBA Enterprises Ltd. Produces a wide range of publications, contract documents and ancilliary materials, on sale at RIBA Bookshops throughout the country.
- RIBA Magazines Ltd. Produces the *RIBA Journal*.
- NBS Services Ltd. An extensive catalogue of specification clauses in standard form.

3 Education Committee

Responsible for:
- Policy proposals on education.
- Monitoring trends in education.
- Examination and qualification arrangements.
- Relationships with schools of architecture.
- Maintenance of agreed regulatory framework.
- Liaison with government and other bodies on educational matters.
- Promotion of architecture as a career.
- Monitoring and promoting equal opportunities in architectural education.

4 Communications Committee

Within the field of communications, to bring committee members' knowledge and experience to bear on issues of policy, priorities and communications expertise.
Responsible for:
- Communications, including relations with RIBA members, government, Parliament, the media, the public, clients and client bodies.
- Awards, partnership funding, architecture gallery, including events and exhibitions at 66 Portland Place.

Activities and functions:
- Advise on the formulation of communications policy and strategy.
- Recommend priorities for the business plan and budget (both income and expenditure).
- Review the implementation of Council policies and the progress of work against agreed objectives.
- Appoint task groups and specialist advisors for relevant projects and subjects.

The Communications Committee is ultimately responsible to the Council of the RIBA and has a direct reporting line to the Council on all major issues of policy.

5 Library Committee

Responsible for:
- Advising on the maintenance and development of the collection.
- Advising on the development of appropriate policies.
- Library accommodation.
- Books, periodicals and drawings.
- Mounting exhibitions.
- Loans to exhibitions.
- Special publications.
- Advising (through the Professional Literature Committee) authors and publishers.
- Publishing the RIBA book list.

6 Membership Committee

Responsible for:
- Development and promotion of all categories of membership worldwide.
- Development and marketing of services for membership worldwide.
- Development of systems designed to facilitate good two-way communications with the membership worldwide.
- Developing the RIBA UK Regional Network and the delivery of services through the regions.
- Relations with other bodies.
- Monitoring the implementation of the Institute's equal opportunities policy re membership.
- Liaising with other main committees and with regional councils.

7 International Relations Committee

Within the area of international affairs, to assist in the formulation of objectives, policy and priorities; ensure effective implementation of Council decisions; and oversee the management of activities.
Responsible for:
- Relations with international organisations including the UIA and CAA, and with national institutes in most countries of the world.
- Relations (on international matters) with UK organisations including BCB, and UKIPG (European/International Forum), plus DETR, DTI and DCMS Creative Industries Export Promotion Group;
- All matters arising from UK membership of the European Union including the Architects' Directive, the Advisory Committee, relations with the European Commission, the Architects' Council of Europe (ACE) and the Comité de Liaison des Architectes Indépendants (CLAI).
- World trade matters relating to overseas provision of services (WTO, GATS, OECD, market access and reciprocal recognition agreements).
- Relations with and services for overseas members.
- All aspects of the RIBA's international role; co-ordination of international work of all departments (Practice, Education and Communications) to ensure consistency of policies.
- Assistance to members seeking work overseas and promoting the RIBA and its members internationally.

8 Disciplinary Committee

Responsible for the administration of the disciplinary procedures. It operates in two separate panels: the Assessment Panel investigates complaints of professional misconduct and, where appropriate, refers cases on to the Hearings Panel via the formulation of a charge. The Hearings Panel interviews members referred to by the Assessment Panel and determines whether or not to reprimand, suspend or expel any member found guilty of breaching the Code of Professional Conduct.

ARCHITECTS REGISTRATION BOARD (ARB)

This is governed by the Architects Act 1997 which provides that all suitably qualified persons must be registered with ARB if they wish to practise under the title of 'architect'.
The principal objectives of ARB are:
- To maintain and publish a register of architects.
- To prescribe admission criteria.
- To protect consumers from misconduct or incompetence.
- To require evidence from firms wishing to use the style 'architect'.
- To draw up a code of conduct.
- To prosecute unregistered persons practising under the title 'architect'.
Membership may be attained:
- By passing prescribed examinations; *and*
- by completing 2 years' practical experience supervised by an architect, one of the years after completing a 5-year course and passing the examinations noted above; *and*
- by passing a written and oral examination, recognised by ARB, in professional practice.

Removal from the register may result from:
- Non-payment of fees.
- Non-notification of change of address.
- A disqualifying decision in another European Economic Area State at the time of registration.
- Unacceptable professional conduct or serious professional incompetence or conviction of criminal offence relevant to fitness to practise.

ARB consists of:
- 7 members after consultation with architects' representative bodies. All registered persons may take part.
- 8 members appointed by the Privy Council to represent the interests of users and the public.

References

ARCHITECT'S HANDBOOK OF PRACTICE MANAGEMENT, pp. 16–18.
THE ARCHITECT IN PRACTICE, pp. 20–4.

Setting up

There are a number of legal obligations that must be taken into consideration when setting up and running an architectural practice. The more important of these affect the office itself and the employment of staff.

Statute 1

Compliance with the Office, Shops and Railway Premises Act 1963

This Act applies to most offices, and affects all 'common parts' e.g. stairs, exits, halls etc. It imposes a duty to register on Form 'OSRI' with the relevant local authority (who, incidentally, will supply the form).

A number of standards are laid down by the Act including cleanliness, overcrowding, temperature of the office, ventilation, lighting, safety and hygiene. Should an accident occur in the office which incapacitates a person for more than 3 days, the local authority must be notified. This applies to injuries to all persons on the premises, not only staff. Compliance with the Act is not required if the staff are self-employed, immediate relatives, or work less than 21 hours per week. Temporary structures are also exempt provided, amongst other things, that they are not used for longer than 6 months. This means that some site offices would be exempt.

Statute 2

Compliance with the Fire Precautions Act 1971

The Act provides that a fire certificate is required for all premises put to designated uses. Among the classes of use which may be designated is use as a place of work. The local fire authority will issue the certificate only if it is satisfied that means of escape and other precautions are such as may be reasonably required. When issued, the fire certificate must specify:

- The use of the premises.
- Means of escape.
- Means with which the building is provided (other than fire-fighting equipment) for ensuring that the means of escape is capable of being safely and effectively used at all material times.
- Type, number and location of all fire-fighting equipment.
- Type, number and location of all means of giving warning in case of fire. An appeal against the contents

of a certificate or the refusal to issue one may be made to the magistrates' court within 21 days.

Statute 3

Compliance with the Health and Safety at Work etc. Act 1974

The main purpose of this Act is to place a duty on every employer to ensure the health, safety and general welfare of employees as far as reasonably possible. This includes keeping a safe work system, giving proper training and (unless fewer than five people are employed) preparing and making known to the staff a statement in writing on the firm's safety policies and arrangements. The employees also have a duty to use reasonable care with regard to themselves and their colleagues. An inspector is empowered to order improvements under this Act, and even to stop the business operating from the offending premises if orders are not complied with. It should be noted that non-compliance amounts to a criminal offence which, therefore, cannot be insured against.

Staff employment

A Stated terms

A contract of employment need not be in writing, but a written contract is preferable as it lessens the risk of misunderstanding. In any event, within 13 weeks of starting a job, a full-time employee must be provided with (or given access to) a statement of terms of the employment.

B Checklist – terms of employment

- Name of parties
- Date on which employment commenced
- Wages or salary rate
- Payment intervals
- Hours to be worked
- Holidays permitted, and holiday pay
- Sickness pay
- Pensions (availability of stakeholder pension scheme)
- Notice
- Job title
- Whether there is a contracting-out certificate in respect of Social Security
- Grievance procedure
- If the employment is for a fixed term, the date when the contract expires.

C Further provisions

When employing architectural staff, consider whether to add any of the following terms:

- Any restrictions on practice after leaving the employment.
- Details of 'perks', e.g. office car.
- Requirements of membership of professional bodies, e.g. RIBA.
- Whether private work is permitted.
- The position as to copyright.
- Professional indemnity arrangement.

D Implied terms

Certain obligations are implied in all contracts of employment. The employer owes a duty to the employee:

- to provide work;
- to pay wages;
- to take reasonable care of the employee's safety;
- to indemnify the employee against liability in the proper performance of their duties.

The employee owes a duty to the employer:

- to act reasonably;
- to work honestly and faithfully, and not to permit personal interest to conflict with their duties;
- to use reasonable skill and care in performing the job, and to indemnify the employer against liability incurred as a result of a breach of this duty.

E Discrimination

It is not permitted to discriminate against an employee, or a prospective employee on the ground of sex or race in Great Britain (although certain limited exceptions apply in relation to sex discrimination). Care should therefore be taken when advertising for staff. It is also not permitted to pay a person a different rate simply because of their sex.

The employer should also consider the position with regard to:

- Rights employees may have to time off work, e.g. maternity leave
- Redundancy legislation
- Legislation on unfair dismissal

References

ARCHITECT'S HANDBOOK OF PRACTICE MANAGEMENT, pp. 137–64.

Communication

Letters

Bear in mind the purpose of the letter, which may be:

TO INFORM
TO RECORD AN EVENT OR CONVERSATION
TO REQUEST INSTRUCTIONS
TO PROMOTE GOOD RELATIONS

This will affect the style of the letter.

- Consider also the impact the letter should have upon the recipient:

    REASSURANCE
    CONFIDENCE
    APPREHENSION
    URGENCY
    FURTHER CONSIDERATION

- Identify the recipient and adopt an appropriate style. For example, do not use technical language of an obscure nature to laymen.
- Avoid 'business jargon'. Phrases like 'we beg to acknowledge' have little meaning and may be irritating to the recipient.
- Be concise, relevant and definite. Wherever possible, keep correspondence to one paragraph. However, if the subject matter merits a lengthy communication, use a separate paragraph for each major point raised or answered. Numbering each point (1.1, 1.2 etc.) will aid future reference.
- End each letter on a positive note by summing up the basic intent of the contents (for example, asking for a response, informing the recipient of the next action to be taken).
- Use the correct form when signing off at the foot of the letter. As a general rule, a letter which opens 'Dear Sir' merits a 'Yours faithfully', and 'Dear Mr X' merits a 'Yours sincerely'. However, less formal phrases may be adopted when parties are better acquainted (e.g. 'With kind regards').
- Check the contents of the finished product before posting for poor grammar, ambiguous phrases, spelling mistakes and typing errors.

Further points

- All letters should ideally be signed by those in authority.
- Incoming letters should be date-stamped and referred to appropriate parties for information or a response.
- It is unwise to enter into correspondence with solicitors where legal action has been indicated, but safer to place the matter in the hands of your own solicitors. However, should this not be necessary or possible, all pre-trial correspondence written with a view to settlement should be headed 'WITHOUT PREJUDICE'. This ensures the letters cannot usually be produced in evidence if the matter gets to court.
- A record of all mail, both sent and received, should be maintained.

Economy tips

- Pre-printed acknowledgement cards are useful in some circumstances, and save the necessity of a letter.
- Window envelopes obviate the need to address a communication twice, and save time.
- Portable dictating machines may also prove useful in saving time, and allow letters or notes to be recorded while still fresh in the mind (for example, on site).
- The development of a computer file or macro for standard letters and/or paragraphs to be used in certain circumstances would save time and provide a consistency of office style.
- As appropriate, mail should be sent by:

    FIRST CLASS POST
    SECOND CLASS POST
    SPECIAL DELIVERY
    RECORDED DELIVERY
    HAND

- Stock both short and long headed notepaper and specify which is required for each letter.
- E-mail is an excellent way to communicate quickly, but be careful. It is not secure, still it constitutes a legal document and is immediate. Sometimes it is better to reflect on a communication before sending it.

Communications

Consider the relative merits of all means of communication relevant to each task.

Communication may be made:

BY LETTER
BY TELEPHONE
BY TELEFAX
BY FAX
BY E-MAIL
BY PERSONAL VISIT

Factors to be taken into consideration when selecting the method of contact include:

- URGENCY
  The telephone is fastest, but e-mail, telex and fax provide written confirmation.
- IMPORTANCE
  Mail may be special or recorded delivery, or, in some cases, delivered by hand.
- ACCURACY
  Written contact is better than oral to impart accurate information.
- CONFIDENTIALITY
  The telephone is person to person and no precise record generally exists.
- DISTANCE
  Long distance calls are expensive, but local calls may be cheaper than postage.
- CONVENIENCE
  Letters require a certain effort in preparation and postage, whereas the telephone provides an instant, simple service.
- EFFICIENCY
  A telephone call may not be practical if it has to be followed by a letter anyway.

Due to the ephemeral nature of its delivery, careful note should be made of all communication involving the telephone. Telephone Attendance Memos facilitate this task.

References

ARCHITECT'S HANDBOOK OF PRACTICE MANAGEMENT, pp. 103–34.
THE ARCHITECT IN PRACTICE, pp. 317–19.

There are currently three standard forms to suit different sizes and complexities of project:

- SFA/99
- CE/99
- SW/99

They have been produced principally for the benefit of architects, to assist in agreement of fees, services and responsibilities. While their use is advisable, the architect is not bound to use them. However, both RIBA and ARB codes (see page 28) require an architect to have clearly set out such matters in writing. It is sensible to include a copy of the appropriate form in early correspondence with a prospective client as a basis for negotiation.

SFA/99 consists of:

- Memorandum of Agreement
- Appendix
- The Schedules
- Services Supplement
- The Conditions
- The Attestation

The Memorandum of Agreement

This identifies the parties, states their intentions and defines the nature, scope and cost of the professional services.

The Appendix

This sets out the applicable law and makes provision to change the limitation period, limit the architect's liability and to appoint an adjudicator and an arbitrator.

The Schedules

Schedule 1

This sets out a description of the client's requirements.

Schedule 2

This sets out the general services to be provided by the architect. There is provision to note which parts of the standard services, such as preparing the design, are to be carried out, together with any other services or special activities, such as interior design and historic buildings work. The Services Supplement is divided into design and management services and a checklist is provided to be deleted as appropriate.

Schedule 3

This sets out the method of calculating and paying fees and expenses and should be read in conjunction with the Conditions. It is divided into the following sections:

- work stage fees
- other fees
- time charge fee hourly rates
- expenses and disbursements
- instalments
- VAT

Schedule 4

This is to be used if consultants, specialists and site staff are to be appointed under separate agreements by the client. It provides for the insertion of names and addresses of the appointees, together with a description of elements to be designed by others.

The Conditions

They are in ten parts:

Definitions

Part 1

This sets out:

- interpretation
- governing law
- communications
- variation to services

Part 2

This sets out the obligations of the architect including appointment of consultants and site visits.

Part 3

This sets out the obligations of the client including provision of information, the CDM Regulations and consultants' responsibilities.

Part 4

This sets out prohibitions on assignment and sub-letting.

Part 5

This sets out detailed provisions for payment. There are essentially three methods of calculating payment:

- percentage of the construction cost
- a lump sum
- a time charge

There are detailed provisions for the payment of additional fees in certain circumstances.

Part 6

This sets out copyright provisions.

Part 7

This sets out liabilities including limitations, PI insurance arrangements and duty of care agreements.

Part 8

This sets out provisions dealing with suspension and termination of services.

Part 9

This sets out the various procedures for dispute resolution:

- negotiation
- conciliation
- adjudication
- arbitration

Codes of Conduct 1

The Codes

Both the RIBA and ARB maintain and enforce Codes of Conduct to which their members are compelled to adhere. The codes are similar in content, and both try to provide a general standard of performance and behaviour in all architects to ensure the best interests of the profession and the public.

The principles embodied in the RIBA code form five sections:
- Principle One
- Principle Two
- Principle Three
- Standard of Professional Performance
- Members' Rules for Clients' Accounts

RIBA Code of Professional Conduct

Principle One

'A member shall faithfully carry out his duties applying his knowledge and experience with efficiency and loyalty towards his client or employer, and being mindful of the interests of those who may be expected to use or enjoy the product of his work.'

This includes:
- Acting impartially in giving advice or acting between parties.
- Stating whether PI insurance is held, defining terms of engagement, scope of service, responsibilities, any limitation of liability, calculation of fees, termination of adjudication provisions.
- Establishing that competence and resources meet the RIBA Standard of Professional Performance and, if an employee, giving due notice to both parties before leaving a post.
- Arranging that an architect is in control of all offices.
- Not sub-contracting services without clients' permission.
- Not abandoning a commission in order to evade responsibilities.

Principle Two

'A member shall, at all times, avoid any action or situation which is inconsistent with his professional obligations or which is likely to raise doubts about his integrity.'

This includes:
- Declaring to prospective clients any business interests which, if undeclared, might raise doubts about the architect's integrity.
- Not continuing in a situation where interests conflict, without the agreement of the other parties.
- Not making or agreeing to any statement which is wrong, contrary to professional opinion, misleading or a discredit to the profession.
- Not simultaneously practising as an independent architect and engaging in certain types of business (trading in land or buildings, property development, auctioneers, estate agents, contracting, sub-contracting or manufacturing goods used in the building industry) unless the firm is clearly identified as distinct from the architectural practice.
- Not purporting to carry out independent architectural functions if the architect (or the architect's employer) is the contractor.
- Not disclosing or using confidential information without the consent of the relevant parties.
- Not accepting discounts, commissions or gifts to show favour to anyone, or allowing the architect's name to be used to endorse a construction product or service.
- Not having as partner or co-director any person who has been expelled from the architect's register, from the RIBA or from any other professional institution.
- Conducting the business in accordance with this principle irrespective of the form of practice of the Companies Acts.
- Notifying the RIBA principal executive officer if becoming insolvent.
- Complying with Members' Rules for Clients' Accounts.

Principle Three

'A member shall in every circumstance conduct himself in a manner which respects the legitimate rights and interests of others.'

This includes:
- Giving no discounts, commissions or gifts to gain clients.
- Not quoting a fee without invitation and sufficient information being provided.
- Not revising a fee quotation to take account of another architect's quotation for the same service.
- Not attempting to supplant another architect.
- Not entering a competition declared unacceptable by the RIBA.
- Not acting in any capacity for work for which the architect had already been appointed a competition assessor.
- Not maliciously or unfairly criticising or discrediting another architect.
- Notifying another architect who has been previously engaged on the same work.
- Notifying another architect if asked to give an opinion on his or her work unless prejudicial to litigation.
- Appropriately acknowledging the contribution of others.
- Defining conditions of employment, authority, responsibility and liability of employees and ensuring waivers of insurer's subrogation rights.
- Reporting any breach of the Code and assisting any investigation unless restricted by the courts.
- Keeping breaches of the Code confidential.
- Reporting to the RIBA if convicted of an indictable criminal offence or if disqualified from acting as a director.

Standard of Professional Performance

'Members are required to maintain in their work and that of their practices a standard of performance which is consistent with membership of the Royal Institute of British Architects and with a proper regard for the interests both of those who commission and those who may be expected to enjoy the product of their work.

Members and their practices will meet the requirements of their engagements with commensurate knowledge and attention so that the quality of the professional services provided does not fall below that which could reasonably be expected of Members of the Royal Institute in good standing in the normal conduct of their business.'

This includes:
- Complying with reasonable instructions, carrying out work diligently, honestly, competently and expeditiously in accordance with agreed timescales and cost limits.
- Fulfilling and allowing employees to fulfil CPD obligations.
- Establishing procedures to ensure clients' complaints are promptly dealt with.
- Arranging for, and notifying clients of, a properly qualified person to run the business while absent.
- Seeking advice on matters outside sphere of knowledge.
- If a sole practitioner, attempting professional contacts to exchange experience and knowledge.
- If a partner or co-director, having regard to capability when delegating.
- Not claiming non-existent expertise or accepting commissions outside sphere of skill and experience.

Members' Rules for Clients' Accounts

Detailed rules for the administration of clients' accounts. A member who is requested to administer an account for a client must confirm in writing the reasons for such administration and the scope of the account. A member is obliged to strictly comply with the rules.

ARB Architects' Code: Standards of Conduct and Practice

Standard 1

'Architects should at all times act with integrity and avoid any action or situations which are inconsistent with their professional obligations.'

Standard 2

'Architects should only undertake professional work for which they are able to provide adequate professional, financial and technical competence and resources.'

Standard 3

'Architects should only promote their professional services in a truthful and responsible manner.'

Standard 4

'Architects should carry out their professional work faithfully and conscientiously and with due regard to relevant technical and professional standards.'

Standard 5

'In carrying out or agreeing to carry out professional work, Architects should pay due regard to the interests of anyone who may reasonably be expected to use or enjoy the products of their work.'

Standard 6

'Architects should maintain their professional service and competence in areas relevant to their professional work, and discharge the requirements of any engagement with commensurate knowledge and attention.'

Standard 7

'Architects should preserve the security of monies entrusted to their care in the course of their practice or business.'

Standard 8

'Architects should not undertake professional work without adequate and appropriate professional indemnity cover.'

Standard 9

'Architects should ensure that their personal and professional finances are managed prudently.'

Standard 10

'An Architect is expected to promote the Standards set out in this Code.'

Standard 11

'Architects should organise and manage their professional work responsibly and with regard to the interests of their clients.'

Standard 12

'Architects should deal with disputes or complaints concerning their professional work or that of their practice of business promptly and appropriately.'

References

ARCHITECT'S HANDBOOK OF PRACTICE MANAGEMENT, pp. 24–30.
THE ARCHITECT IN PRACTICE, pp. 27–34.

The Employer

Type

The architect/employer relationship will be affected by the type of employer particular to each commission. The employer could be:

    A PRIVATE INDIVIDUAL
    A PARTNERSHIP
    A CORPORATION OR INSTITUTION
    A LOCAL OR CENTRAL GOVERNMENT
    DEPARTMENT
    A SOCIETY

NOTE: Some contracts will involve dealing with both an employer and a 'user', e.g. in a school project, the Education Authority is usually the employer, and the teaching staff are the users. Care should be taken not to confuse the roles.

Effect

The relationship will also be influenced by the character of the project itself. Factors which may be affected include:

- the architect/employer agreement
- tendering procedures
- type of building contract
- statutory approvals required
- use of nominated sub-contractors
- methods of communication (e.g. who is responsible to whom within the respective organisations)

Contact

The initial contact with the employer may be made:

- by recommendation
- by reputation (a general excellence or a specialisation)
- by competition work
- by previous contact
- by employer interest in architect's previous work
- by employer interest in architect's current work
- by chance
- through RIBA Client Advisory Service

The agreement

The form of agreement between the architect and the employer is very important. Oversights or omissions at this stage could lead to problems later in the project which foresight and attention to detail might have prevented. There are a number of ways in which the relationship can be formalised:

- by conduct of the parties (see page 51)
- by letter (see page 33)
- by RIBA Memorandum of Agreement (see page 31)
- by memorandum of agreement as a deed (giving a 12-year liability period)
- by employer's own form

Changes

If the standard clauses in the Memorandum of Agreement have to be altered, supplemented or omitted, great care should be taken to ensure that the architect's liability is not adversely affected. The provisions of the Unfair Contract Terms Act 1977 should also be noted, as they may render some terms void in certain instances. It is advisable to comply with the conditions set out in the SFA 99 (see page 27) which should be attached to, and form part of, the final agreement with the employer.

Contents

All agreements should include:

- details of the extent and purpose of the project;
- the general nature of the agreement;
- details of the site (location and address);
- the responsibilities and roles of the parties;
- methods of calculating fees and expenses;
- times and amounts of payments;
- details of full and partial services;
- additional services, if any;
- other matters discussed (consultants, type of contract, etc.).

Checklist: Stage A Appraisal

Factors to be considered at preliminary meetings, and possibly mentioned in letters of acceptance and/or forms of agreement may include:

Obtain details of:

- client and representative (names, addresses, etc.)
- project
- site
- proposed user

Check:

- the seriousness of the employer and their financial position;
- whether any other architects are involved (if so, inform them of your position);
- the availability of office resources, etc.;
- statutory requirements, consents, etc.

Discuss:

- appointment and payment of consultants;
- type of procurement path and of contract to be used;
- methods of tendering;
- early appointment of contractor, sub-contractors and suppliers;
- methods of insurance and assurance (bonds, warranties etc.);
- limitation of liability.

Provide the client with:

- a copy of SFA 99, applicable scale fees and details of payment stages;
- name of the architect to be in charge of the project and methods of communication.

References

THE ARCHITECT'S GUIDE TO RUNNING A JOB, pp. 2–9
ARCHITECT'S HANDBOOK OF PRACTICE MANAGEMENT, pp. 182–4.
THE ARCHITECT IN PRACTICE, pp. 81–153.

is Agreement

is made the _____6th_____ day of _November_ (month) 2001_____ (year)

BETWEEN

HUSSEIN CHARGEER_____
of (or whose registered office is situated at)

1, LETSBY AVENUE, CRINGING, WILTS_____

_____ ('the Client')

AND

FAIR AND SQUARE_____
of (or whose registered office is situated at)

4, THE HELLOVET, CRINGING, WILTS_____

_____ ('the Architect')

ecital

Whereas

The Client has requested the Architect to perform professional services in relation to:

THE CONSTRUCTION OF A PRIVATE DWELLING_____

at _1, LETSBY AVENUE, CRINGING, WILTS_____ ('the Site')
as described in Schedule 1 to this Agreement ('the Project').

rticles

It is agreed that:

1 The appointment is made and accepted on the Articles, the Conditions, the Appendix and the Schedules hereto which together comprise the Agreement.

2 The Client hereby appoints the Architect and the Architect hereby accepts the appointment for the Project and will perform the Services set out in Schedule 2 to this Agreement.

3 The Client undertakes to carry out his duties in accordance with this Agreement and to pay the Architect the fees, expenses and disbursements specified in Schedule 3 to this Agreement.

4 The Client has appointed or will appoint the Consultants and others listed in Schedule 4 to this Agreement to perform services in connection with the Project.

5 Without prejudice to any right of adjudication, any dispute or difference arising out of this Agreement shall be referred to:

(unless otherwise stated) Arbitration in accordance with the Conditions
~~or legal proceedings~~

6 The Effective Date[1] of this Agreement shall be:

_____8th_____ day of _November_____ (month)___2001_____(year)

[1] Unless otherwise stated, the date on which the Architect commenced performance of the Services

Appendix to the Conditions

Clauses		
1.3	The law applicable to this contract shall be the law of:	England
7.2 and 7.4	Time limit[2] for action or proceedings and insurance cover: [2] Unless otherwise stated, 6 years (or 12 years if executed as a Deed)	Six years
7.3.1 and 7.4	Limit of liability and amount[3] of Professional Indemnity Insurance cover: [3] Unless otherwise stated, PII cover, excluding legal costs, will be not less than the amount required by the Architects Registration Board	£ 100,000
9.4	The Adjudicator shall be[4] : Not applicable of _____ [4] Insert name, 'agreed or nominated', or 'not applicable'	

Where no Adjudicator is named in the Agreement, or the named Adjudicator is unable or unwilling to act, the nominator shall be:

(unless otherwise stated) the President of the Royal Institute of British Architects

or *(other)* _____

| 9.5 | Where Arbitration is chosen, the appointor shall be: | |

(unless otherwise stated) the President of the Royal Institute of British Architects

or *(other)* _____

☆ ACME ☆
SERVICES LTD

March 8th

Dear Sir,
I am at present engaged in negotiations involving a development in this area. Your firm has been recommended to me and, should you be interested, I would like you to start work as soon as possible on my behalf. Please phone my secretary and make an appointment for next Thursday (tel. 01765 2230).

Yours faithfully,

B. Wiley

B.Wiley
Managing Director

MEMO

To : B. Fair
    : T. Square
From : 4th Mar.
Date :
Concerning : New technican.

I have interviewed D. Taylor for the position and am satisfied. Could you draft out a letter of appointment, as I shall be away this week. Vicki has a note of the terms discussed.

Tom.

CRINGING BOROUGH COUNCIL

Town Clerk:
S. Topple.

Our ref: ST/cf/80/876

The Town Hall,
Cringing.

4.3.02

Dear Sirs,

re: Proposed Day Care Centre, Cringing

I write following our recent meeting, when you met members of the appropriate committee and discussed the above scheme in broad outline.

My Council will be meeting next week to formalise your appointment as Architects for the project, and I should like to be able to put before them your full proposals in regard to your fees and Conditions of Engagement.

You will appreciate that, should my Council accept your proposals, they will form a contract for services and I therefore rely upon you to explain everything which you consider to be a necessary part of such a contract.

I look forward to your early reply.

Yours faithfully,

S. Topple

S.Topple
Town Clerk

11th March

Dear Tom,
Janet and I have decided to extend the house and add a granny flat for her Mother.

As our neighbour, we would like you to draw up t plans. Will it cost much, and when could you start?

See you this weekend,

Regards,

Sam Evenin

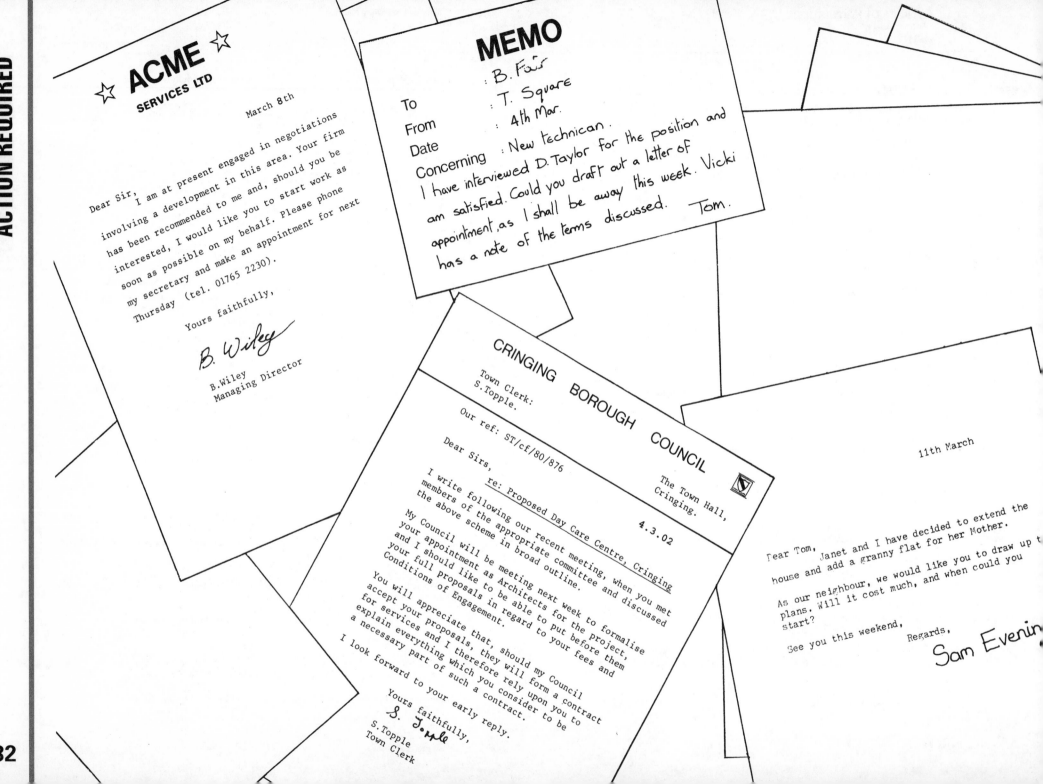

MEMO

: Bill F.

: Tom Sq.

: 12.3.02

: Work for Friend.

...erning ...y neighbour Sam wants us to do his ...tension. I think we'd better not, and besides, ...re pretty busy at the moment—can you suggest ...neone reliable to refer him to? T.S.

A Mr. O. Pforagh-Nuther has asked us to do a new house for him. next to ... Have used a Memo of Agreement on ...his request.

Fair and Square

B.FAIR.dip.arch.RIBA.
T.SQUARE.B.Arch.RIBA.AFAS.

CHARTERED ARCHITECTS

BF/vn

4, The Hellovet,
Cringing,
Wilts.

6.MAR.02

Dear Mr Topple,

re: Proposed Day Care Centre, Cringing.

Thank you for your letter of the 4th March. We are pleased to note that your Council is considering our firm to act as architects in the above project, and write to confirm the terms under which we could accept the commission.

The RIBA Standard Form of Agreement currently in use (a copy of which we append to this letter) sets out the conditions upon which members of the Institute operate and the services which are offered.

We confirm that we are willing to work on a percentage fee of x%, which we feel is appropriate to this type of project. If work on a time basis is required, it will be based upon a charge of £x per hour for principal's time and an hourly rate of y pence per £100 of gross annual income for technical staff.

Should your Council decide to employ us, we recommend the use of the Memorandum of Agreement published by the RIBA (two copies of which we enclose) to formalise the appointment, unless you prefer to use a similar document of your own.

Should you require any further information, please do not hesitate to contact us, and we look forward to hearing from you in the near future.

Your sincerely,

and Square

...arch.RIBA.
.B.Arch.RIBA.AFAS.

CHARTERED ARCHITECTS

Dear Mr Taylor,

re: Appointment as Architectural Technician

Further to your recent discussion with my partner, Tom Square, on the 4th March, we are pleased to confirm that we have decided to appoint you as technician to this firm. As agreed, we would like you to commence work on May 6th.

4, The Hellovet
Cringing,
Wilts.

5.MAR.02

Your salary, details of which appear on the attached sheet, will be paid on the 1st of each calendar month. Working hours are 9.15 am to 5.00 pm Monday to Friday, with an hour for lunch. Initially you will be entitled to 4 weeks' paid holiday, exclusive of statutory holidays. Payment in respect of time off for illness, details of our pension scheme, notice, contracting-out certificates and procedures in the event of grievances are all dealt with on the attached procedure sheet, which you are asked to read carefully and retain.

...a condition of your employment, we would require prior notice ...d you wish to undertake any private commissions.

...the foregoing is clear, but if you should be in doubt on ...er, please let us know. Tom and I look forward to working...

Yours sincerely,
B. Fair for
Fair & Square

Fair and Square

MEMO

To

From : Tom

Date : Bill

: 12 th March

Concerning : Acme Services Ltd:— What a vague Letter! Are we dealing with Mr. Wiley personally or his company? Suggest we ask for further details be... commiting ourselves, plus make guarded enqu... about his standing. Should we go a... Let's ask for a fair-sized adv... to test him out.

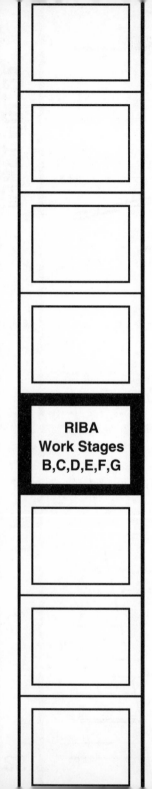

THE DESIGN PHASE

Contents

RIBA
Work Stages
B,C,D,E,F,G

Certain legal rights and constraints regarding land may affect
  a) the choice of site for a particular development, or
  b) the character of the development if the site is already determined.
The more important of these constraints are examined here.

Land

The major characteristics of land are:
- A. TENURE, the duration of tenant's rights
- B. REGISTRATION

A TENURE
A tenant's rights in land are categorised as:
        FREEHOLD
        LEASEHOLD
Freehold property enables the owner to retain full possession of the absolute title of the land for an uncertain duration.

Leasehold property enables the lessee to retain enjoyment of the land, subject to the terms of the lease, for a specified number of years only. (On new leases, this may be as long as 999 years, although much shorter leases, particularly in central London, are common, e.g. 25 years.)

Multi-occupancy dwellings must be sold leasehold, where leaseholders pay a specified fee (ground rent) to the freeholder.

B REGISTRATION
The Land Registration Act 1925 led to the compulsory registration of land on the register maintained by the Land Registry upon transfer in a number of regions. Searching for incumbrances (e.g. restrictive covenants) on registered land is therefore less perilous than for unregistered land. Care should be taken to consult with all necessary Land Charges Registers. For both registered and unregistered land however, searches are made in the relevant district offices.

There are a number of legal characteristics relevant to property that may influence or affect building proposals. The more important of these are:
- boundaries
- easements
- covenants
- trespass

Boundaries

These can be determined:
- by examination of the title deeds;
- by order of certain authorities;

- by presumption, where no definition can be traced. Examine walls and fences (e.g. fences in built-up areas are presumed to be built on the land of the person who erected them, so that the boundaries are determined by the smooth face of the fence, where the boundary posts are fixed to the other side). Legitimacy may depend upon providing 12 years' uninterrupted use.

Care must be taken that all boundaries are settled by the client's solicitor.

Easements

Easements are legal rights enjoyed by one party over the land of another. They can be acquired in four ways:
- by statute, if specifically mentioned;
- expressly, that is, by deed;
- impliedly, by necessity (e.g. support);
- by prescription, persons using property in some way may be considered to have certain common law rights if they have enjoyed them for a long period (usually 20 years).

Types of easement

- RIGHTS OF WAY
  These may be limited as to type of user or frequency of use.
- RIGHTS OF SUPPORT
  From adjoining property.
- RIGHTS OF LIGHT
  Daylight regulations now fall under planning law and the Rights of Light Act 1959.

Easements are not necessary for:
- natural rights, like support of land (but not building);
- public rights, e.g. right of way over a highway.

Covenants

Restrictive covenants concern the prevention of certain actions of specific property, although much of this area is now limited by planning law. A restrictive covenant may be used, for example, by a developer to prevent the growing of hedges or the building of fences by future owners on a housing estate. Care should be taken not to transgress any existing restrictive covenants by new work.

Trespass

Unauthorised entry onto the land of another (including the air space to a reasonable height above and the soil beneath) may give the owner cause for an action for trespass. For example, trees overhanging a neighbour's property constitute a technical trespass, and the latter may lop the branches with impunity. Intruding roots below ground may be destroyed and, if they cause damage, may result in a civil action against the tree owner. Eaves projection over adjoining property is also trespass, and an express licence should be sought to obtain a right of 'eavesdrop'.

Trespass may be:
- temporary, e.g. walking over the property;
- permanent, e.g. building a wall over the boundary line.

If it becomes necessary to enter a neighbour's land for any reason (e.g. to facilitate building operations), a temporary licence should be negotiated with the owner to avoid trespass. In the case of trespass upon a building site, it usually remains the contractor's responsibility to ensure the security of the land and the equipment upon it. Damage, even to trespassers, may be considered the fault of the contractor if the site is found to be dangerous and measures of protection considered to be inadequate. Particular care is necessary where children are concerned, as child trespassers are considered to merit a higher degree of care. See Occupiers Liability Act 1984 Section 1 (3).

Nuisance

Further consideration of the neighbour's rights must be given if the adjoining property is used for some anti-social or potentially dangerous purpose.

Nuisance may be:
- public, a criminal offence;
- private, a tort involving interference with the enjoyment of land. An example of this would be excessive noise, dust or smell. If a neighbour is seriously inconvenienced, a suit for nuisance to prevent the offending usage or to obtain damages may result.

References

ARCHITECT'S LEGAL HANDBOOK, pp. 4, 29–37, 42–6.
LAW, pp. 241–71.

Brief Development

Stage B: Strategic briefing

Stage B entails the development of a more detailed investigation and appreciation of the employer's requirements and the constraints and conditions that affect them.

Considerations

Factors affecting the project include:
- the type of building (size, character);
- the quality required;
- special conditions (e.g. future flexibility);
- time available;
- finance available (for both the construction of the project and its running costs when operational).

Effects

Careful consideration should be given at this point, as the combination of the previous factors may influence, among other things:
- the method of tendering;
- the type of contract;
- use of bonus/liquidated damages clauses;
- early appointment of the contractor/sub-contractors;
- employment of the quantity surveyor/other consultants;
- cost studies;
- studies and work outside the architect's normal services;
- methods of assurance (insurance, bond etc.).

Procedure

Physical constraints and the integration of the accommodation requirements will be better understood after the preparation of an adequate schedule of accommodation and a site survey.

Accommodation brief

The primary accommodation brief should include details of:
- overall project requirements (function and character of spaces, their juxtaposition, areas and room heights, relationship of internal and external spaces);
- primary elements (walls, roofs, floors, etc.);
- secondary elements (materials, windows, doors, special features, etc.);
- internal and external features;
- services to be included;
- installations and lighting (artificial and natural);
- fixtures;
- other special requirements, e.g. special equipment or furniture.

Building survey checklist

Factors to consider when surveying property may include, but are not limited to, the following:
- WALLS (EXTERNAL)
- CHECK: Brickwork (cracks), pointing (crumbling), render (cracks, bulges, flaking), DPCs (bridging) and airbricks (blockages)
- WALLS (INTERNAL)
- CHECK: Plaster (cracks, bulges, damp patches)
- ROOF
- CHECK: Tiles, slates (cracks, weathering, slippage). Hip, ridge and valley tiles. Flashings. Roof space and rafters (damp, rot, leaks). Flat roof skirtings, upstands and flashings.
- ELECTRIC/GAS
- CHECK: Fittings, cables, pipes and supply joints
- PLUMBING
- Hot and cold water systems (pipes, valves, joints, cisterns and fittings)
- DRAINAGE
- CHECK: Drains, gulleys, manholes, rodding eyes, fittings (cracks, blockages)
- RAINWATER GOODS
- CHECK: Gutters, downpipes and outlets (blockages and leaks), hoppers (blockages)
- FITTINGS
- CHECK: Cupboards, units etc.
- FLOORS AND CEILINGS
- CHECK: Woodwork, cills, lintels (leaks and rot)
- EXTERNAL WORK
- CHECK: Soil, paving etc. (keep below DPC level). Drainage of surface water (away from house). Position of trees and bushes near house

Site surveys

- Check with the employer and/or the local authority or the employer's legal agents as to title, and any restrictions affecting development, e.g. covenants, easements, boundaries, rights of adjoining neighbours, etc.
- Check all legal requirements (planning, building control, etc.) and establish whether any special permissions are necessary (for example, from the licensing justices), or whether any particular restrictions apply, e.g. listed building or conservation areas (see page 37).
- Check the employer's existing site information, and establish its accuracy.
- Determine the need and extent of a new survey, e.g. whether it should be outline or full.
- Decide whether to consult specialists, e.g. soils engineer.
- Check access to the site, and procure maps to establish boundaries, etc., upon which mark details of boundaries, buildings and special features of adjoining land.
- Where necessary, survey the buildings on site (plans, elevations and sections, position on site and assessment of condition).
- Note special features, general topography and landscape, including tree types and whether they are subject to Tree Preservation Orders (a full site survey may involve taking levels and a detailed site measurement).
- Note orientation and any obvious meteorological factors.
- Record roads (use, traffic flow etc.), paths and routes in and around the site.
- Record services existing on and near to the site, and note their ownership and capacity (the local authority may be able to assist). Invert levels may be useful. Also, note the connections.
- Make a general assessment of all features and structures on the site, and note any general observations.
- Sketches and/or a photographic record of the site and surrounding area may prove useful for quick reference back at the office.

At the beginning of any project, attention should be paid to the various legal constraints that may affect the scheme. Some will apply to all projects, e.g. planning and building control, whereas others will only be relevant to certain types of schemes, e.g. the provision of the Fire Precautions Act 1971. Furthermore, some regulations will only apply to projects in particular localities:

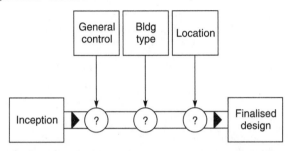

General constraints

Nearly all building operations require planning permission (see page 38) and building regulations approval (see page 42). Most schemes also demand consideration by the architect of services availability, and the position of the employer with regard to the statutory undertakers, i.e. gas supplier, water supplier, sewage and highways authorities, electricity supplier, etc. In most cases there is a right to connection to main services, but the position should be checked for each particular case. The relevant statutes are:
- for sewers: Public Health Act 1936;
- for water: Water Act 1945;
- for gas: Gas Act 1972;
- for electricity: Electricity Act 1947.

Statutory undertakers have wide powers to lay services on private land without consent, provided that compensation is paid.

The appropriate telephonic communications provider should be contacted with regard to the installation of telephones.

Types of project

Particular projects are sometimes affected by specific legal constraints, e.g. the construction of a factory must be in accordance with the Factories Act 1961 and comply with the Clean Air Acts 1956 and 1968. Drainage from a factory or other trade premises must conform with the Public Health (Drainage of Trade Premises) Act 1937.

In any premises put to designated uses a fire certificate is required under the Fire Precautions Act 1971 (see page 25), and nearly all businesses are affected by the Offices, Shops and Railway Premises Act 1963, and the Health and Safety at Work Etc. Act 1974 (see page 25). Certain types of proposed business premises require licences to enable them to operate, e.g. petrol stations, pubs, restaurants, music and dance halls, cinemas, abattoirs, nursing homes, etc. The relevant statutes for these example are:
- petrol stations: Petroleum Consolidation Act 1928;
- pubs and restaurants: Licensing Acts 1953 and 1964
- music and dance halls: Public Health Acts (Amendment Act) 1890;
- cinemas: Cinematograph Acts 1909 and 1952;
- abattoirs: Slaughterhouses Act 1974;
- nursing homes: Nursing Homes Act 1975.

This list is not exhaustive, and investigation should always be made regarding the construction and licensing requirements in respect of the use proposed.

ODPs and IDCs

Office Development Permits (ODPs) and Industrial Development Certificates (IDCs) are not currently required, although it should be noted that conditions relating to existing planning permissions are still in force.

Locality

Some restrictions affect all projects within a specified area, e.g. proposed projects within conservation areas must satisfy additional considerations in order to obtain planning permission. Some areas are subject to Smoke Control Orders which limit the type of fuel which can be used for domestic heating systems. Restrictions of this nature may be discovered by making the relevant enquiries of the local authority.

In addition, designated Urban Development Areas and Enterprise Zones will have special requirements which must be investigated.

Grants

In certain cases grants may be available to assist in the cost of development.

Types of grant include:
- improvement grant
- intermediate grant
- repairs grant
- special grant

In addition financial assistance may be available in respect of:
- insulation
- water connection
- listed buildings
- compliance with Clean Air legislation
- water closets
- certain agricultural development

A comprehensive analysis of the types of grants available can be found in *The Architect's Legal Handbook* (7th Edition).

References

THE ARCHITECT IN PRACTICE, pp. 135–45.
THE ARCHITECT'S GUIDE TO RUNNING A JOB, pp. 32–5, 54–5.
ARCHITECT'S LEGAL HANDBOOK, pp. 169–80, 184–2111.
ARCHITECT'S HANDBOOK OF PRACTICE MANAGEMENT, pp. 282–6.

Planning

Planning law

The enactments of current planning law are consolidated in four Acts:
- The Town and Country Planning Act 1990
- The Planning (Listed Buildings and Conservation Areas) Act 1990
- The Planning (Hazardous Substances) Act 1990
- The Planning (Consequential Provisions) Act 1990

Some procedures have been modified by The Planning and Compensation Act 1991. One of the major powers vested in each planning authority is the production of development plans for future growth. The development plan is of two types:
- the Unitary Development Plans in the London boroughs and metropolitan districts;
- the Structure Plan prepared by county councils and the Local Plans prepared by district councils containing detailed local policies and proposals for the district.

Prior to any detailed scheme design, the architect should check the development plan and assess its relevance, if any, to the project in hand.

The architect should also check:
- if the site of the proposed development is within a Conservation Area;
- if any buildings on the site have been considered to be of special architectural and/or historical interest, in which case, they will be Listed and Graded;
- if any trees on the site are subject to Tree Preservation Orders.

This information can all be discovered in the local planning authorities' offices.

Planning permission

Before applying for planning permission, further checks regarding the development itself should be made:
- Does the work constitute 'development'? Check the Town and Country Planning Act 1990.
- If it does form development, is it 'permitted development'? Check the Town and Country Planning General Development Orders.

If the preliminary checks indicate that the development will require planning permission, application should be made on the appropriate forms. There are two kinds of planning permission: Outline or Full.

Outline

This is a useful device to 'test the water', and check the feasibility of a project before too much work has been done. If granted, it shows the authority's approval in principle. Often, only limited information is required, but in some cases (e.g. Conservation Areas), the authority may request additional data.

Full

This gives the successful applicant freedom to undertake the proposals indicated in the submitted documents.

Documents in support of an application for full planning permission include:
- the completed forms
- the required fee
- the drawings (site plan, layout plan and building plans)
- certificate of ownership (A, B, C, or D)

The information necessary includes:
- address of the site
- name and address of owner
- type of development
- means of drainage (foul and surface water)
- area of development
- storage of hazardous materials
- employment (existing and proposed)
- parking spaces
- present site use
- highway access
- permanent/temporary development
- description of materials (including colour)
- position of major areas, and their relationship to other buildings, trees, etc.
- details of the proposal (plans, elevations)

According to the type of development and its location, other constraints may have to be taken into consideration (see page 37). The application may be published in the local press and a decision made by the planning authorities, usually within 2 months.

The application may be:
- granted;
- granted subject to conditions (temporary or permanent);
- refused. Reasons must be given for refusal, and an appeal may be made (see page 41).

If permission is granted (in any form) work must begin on site within 5 years (or other specified period). If the land is sold within that time, planning permission remains valid unless it is personal to the applicant (which is rare).

Completion Notice

If it is clear that the work will not be finished within a reasonable time, a COMPLETION NOTICE may be served. This comes into force after a period of not less than one year from the date of the notice, when all work shown on the approved drawings which is not completed loses planning permission.

Enforcement Notice

If development is started without permission, or without regard to the conditions imposed, the authority may service an ENFORCEMENT NOTICE, ordering the party in violation to take the necessary steps to ensure compliance with the planning requirements. There is a route of appeal to the Secretary of State within 28 days.

Stop Notice

An ENFORCEMENT NOTICE may be followed by a STOP NOTICE, halting all work under penalty of a heavy fine. It may also be used to stop changes of use (if it is served within a year, and the change is not to a single dwelling house).

Planning Contravention Notice

A procedure under which the planning authority can obtain information. The recipient has 21 days to reply.

Breach of Conditions Notice

The planning authority may require compliance in 28 days with a planning condition. There is no appeal.

References

ARCHITECT'S LEGAL HANDBOOK, pp. 255–79.
MAKING YOUR PLANNING APPEAL (1999), The Planning Inspectorate.

Please read the accompanying notes before completing any part of this form.

APPLICATION FOR PERMISSION TO DEVELOP LAND ETC.

Town and Country Planning Act 1990

Four completed copies of this form and 5 copies of all plans accompanying the application must be submitted to the Planning Department of the District Council in which the land which is the subject of this application is situated; the fifth copy may be retained by the applicant for information.

For office use only
Ref.
Date received

PART 1—to be completed by or on behalf of all applicants as far as applicable to the particular development.   Please answer all questions.

1. Applicant (in block capitals)

Name HUSSEIN CHARGEER ESQ

Address 1 LETSBY AVENUE

CRINGING, WILTS

Tel. No. (010)01010   Applicant's interest in land OWNER

Agent (if any) to whom correspondence should be sent (in block capitals)

Name FAIR AND SQUARE

Address 4, THE HELLOVET

CRINGING, WILTS

Tel. No. (010) 10101

2. Particulars of proposal for which permission or approval is sought

(a) Full address or location of the land to which this application relates and site area.

1 LETSBY AVENUE, CRINGING, WILTS

Site Area   0·7   ~~*Yards²/Metres²~~ ~~Acres~~/Hectares   *Delete where appropriate

(b) Brief particulars of proposed development including the purpose(s) for which the land and/or buildings are to be used

NEW HOUSE IN GROUNDS OF APPLICANT'S PRESENT DWELLING TO BE USED BY SAME

Gross floor space of building if 1000 sq.m. or over   —   sq.m.

(c) State whether applicant owns or controls any adjoining land and if so, give its location   NO

(d) State whether the proposal involves:—

		State Yes or No		Yes or No
* (i)	Work connected with a building destroyed or demolished not more than 10 years ago	NO	If the answer is 'yes' will the proposed gross floor space be not more than 10% of original building.	
* (ii)	Alteration, extension or improvement	NO		
* (iii)	New building(s)	YES		1 HOUSE

(*If residential development, state number of dwelling units proposed and type if known, e.g. houses, bungalows, flats)

		State Yes or No	
(iv)	Change of use	NO	
(v)	Construction of a new access to a highway vehicular	YES	If development does not involve construction of new access or alteration of existing access, please give details of existing access.
	pedestrian	YES	
(vi)	Alteration of an existing access to a highway vehicular	NO	
	pedestrian	NO	

3. Particulars of Application (see note 3)

		State Yes or No	
(a)	State whether this application is for:—		
(i)	Outline planning permission	NO →	If yes, delete any of the following which are not reserved for subsequent approval
(ii)	Full planning permission	YES	

1 siting   3 external appearance

2 design   4 means of access

		State Yes or No	
(iii)	Approval of reserved matters following the grant of outline permission	NO →	If yes, state the date and number of outline permission Date Number
(iv)	Renewal of a temporary permission or permission for retention of building or continuance of use without complying with a condition subject to which planning permission has been granted	NO →	If yes, state the date and number of previous permission and identify the particular condition (see note 3d). Date Number The condition

Note: Forms vary considerably between authorities

Form App. 1

4. **Particulars of Present and Previous Use of Buildings or Land**

State

   (i)   Present use of ~~buildings~~/land   (i) PART OF OWNER'S GARDEN

   (ii)   If vacant, the last previous use   (ii) —

5. **Additional Information**

   (a)   Is the application for Industrial, office, warehousing, storage or shopping purposes? (See note 5)

State Yes or No

| NO |

If yes, complete Part 2 of this form

   (b)   Does the proposed development involve the felling of any trees?

State Yes or No

| NO |

If yes, indicate positions on plan

   (c)   (i)   How will surface water be disposed of?

         (ii)   How will foul sewage be dealt with?

(i) LOCAL AUTHORITY SURFACE WATER MAINS

(ii) Tick as appropriate

- [✓] Mains
- [ ] Septic tank (see (c) (iii) below)
- [ ] Cesspit (see Note 11)
- [ ] Other

         (iii) If septic tank drainage, does the development involve more than one dwelling using a single septic tank (either existing or proposed?)

- [ ] Yes
- [ ] No

   (d)   What is the proposed water supply for this development?

Tick as appropriate

- [✓] Public Mains
- [ ] Private. If private water supply, has the applicant received written permission from the owner to connect to that supply?
  - [ ] Yes
  - [ ] No

   (e)   If the application involves a new building or extension please state the materials

      (i) Roof   (i) SLATES

      (ii) Walls   (ii) BRICKS

6. **Plans**

List of drawings and plans submitted with the application   8072/01,02,03,04,05

Note: *The proposed means of enclosure, the materials and colour of the walls and roof, landscaping details etc. should be clearly shown on the submitted plans, unless the application is in outline only*

I/We hereby apply for

   *(a)   planning permission to carry out the development described in this application and the accompanying plans, and in accordance therewith.

   ~~OR *(b) planning permission to retain building or works or continue a use without complying with a condition already imposed on an earlier planning permission on this application and the accompanying plans.~~

   ~~OR *(c) approval of details of buildings or works already begun or carried out in anticipation of the planning permission sought in this application and the accompanying plans.~~

* Delete whichever is not applicable.

Date   22 February 2002

Signed   *Fair & Square*

On behalf of   HUSSEIN CHARGEER ESQ

(Insert applicants name if signed by an agent)

A planning appeal may be made in respect of a number of matters, including enforcement notices (within 28 days of notice), cases where it is doubtful whether permission is needed and established use certificates. However, the most common type is made because permission has not been granted in the terms of the application. Thus appeals may be made against:

- the refusal of permission;
- conditions imposed upon approval;
- failure of the planning authorities to make a decision within 8 weeks, or within an agreed extension period;
- refusal of the planning authorities to approve details reserved at the granting of outline permission;
- conditions attached to such details;
- failure of the authorities to make a decision in respect of an application for approval of details within 8 weeks.

Appeal can only be made by the person who made the original application, or an agent acting on their behalf. Notice of appeal (in the appropriate form) must be given to the Secretary of State for the DETR. The time limit to make an appeal varies from 28 days to 6 months from the planning authority's decision, depending on the reason for the appeal.

Procedure

Appeal applications should comprise the following documents:
- two copies of the appeal form (which states the grounds of the appeal);
- a copy of the original planning application;
- copies of any certificates relating to ss. 26 and 27 of the 1971 Act, and copies of other relevant certificates or permits (e.g. Office Development Permit);
- copies of plans, drawings and documents submitted with the original planning application;
- a copy of the authority's decision;
- a copy of the outline permission (if the appeal refers to an application for approval of details);
- copies of all pertinent correspondence between the parties.

The appeal

There are three ways of dealing with an appeal:
- without an inquiry;
- by a public local inquiry;
- by an informal hearing.

Without an inquiry

The appeal, known as a written representation, is sent to the planning authority for a statement upon which the appellant may comment. The case is then decided by the Secretary of State or, more usually, by a designated inspector, who may, in many cases, visit the site prior to delivering a decision in writing.

Public local inquiry

This would be chaired by an inspector appointed by the Secretary of State, where the appellant and the planning authorities have requested that the matter be dealt with at a local level.

Informal hearing

This is a simplified procedure having some of the characteristics of 'written representations' and 'public local inquiry'.

Normally, each side in an inquiry pays its own costs, but the Secretary of State may order one party to pay all or part of the other's costs as well as its own.

Listed buildings

Listed Building Consent – Appeals Against Refusal (The Planning (Listed Buildings and Conservation Areas) Act 1990)

This information is largely applicable where an appeal is made against a refusal by the planning authorities to allow demolition within a conservation area, or alteration or demolition of a listed building.

When considering such an appeal, the Secretary of State will pay special attention to:
- the importance of the building, both on its own and in relation to others (listed buildings only);
- the condition of the building;
- the importance of any alternative use for the site;

and additionally, where the building is in a conservation area:
- the probable effect on the character and appearance of the area.

Definition of 'development'

For a complete description of what constitutes 'development', see Section 55 of the Town and Country Planning Act 1990. The situation is by no means always simple.

Briefly, 'development' means:
- the carrying out of building, engineering, mining or other operations in, on, over or under land;
- the making of any material change in the use of any buildings or other land.

Not all 'development' requires planning permission.

'Permitted development'

'Permitted development' (i.e. operations which constitute 'development' but for which express permission need not be sought) is detailed in the Town and Country Planning General Development Orders. Examples are:
- certain enlargements etc. of dwelling houses (erection of garages within their curtilages is 'enlargement' under this Order);
- erection of gates, walls and fences;
- building operations for agricultural purposes on agricultural land;
- erection of most temporary buildings, e.g. site huts, provided they are removed at the expiration of the operations which they serve;
- certain local authority construction and alterations;
- certain development by statutory undertakers.

Permitted development rights can be removed by conditions on a planning permission or by a subsequent Direction of the Town and Country Planning General Development Orders.

References

MAKING YOUR PLANNING APPEAL (1999), The Planning Inspectorate.

Building Control 1

Building control

Building control is a function delegated to the local authorities in England and Wales, where the Building Regulations, created under the Building Act 1984, are implemented by building control officers or approved inspectors. (In Scotland, similar provisions are made by the Building (Scotland) Acts.) These are illustrated fully in THE BUILDING REGULATIONS, 1999, Chapters 1–4.

The Building Regulations

The regulations are designed to secure the health, safety, welfare and convenience of persons in or about buildings, furthering the conservation of fuel and power and preventing waste, undue consumption, misuse and the contamination of water. In most cases, where an individual wishes to build or make alterations to a building, the appropriate authorities must be notified. However, the applicant should first check to see if the proposed development is exempted from the regulations (see Table A). The requirements of the regulations are generally expressed in functional terms and are supported by a series of Approved Documents. However, compliance may be gained by reference to other documents, such as British Standards.

Relaxations/dispensations

If the regulations apply but seem unnecessarily onerous, a RELAXATION or DISPENSATION may be sought from the local authority (or Secretary of State). The procedure may be found in the Building Act 1984, and appeals can be made to the Secretary of State if the authority refuses an application for a relaxation. TYPE RELAXATIONS may also be granted by the Secretary of State under provisions enacted in the Building Act 1984, which can dispense with regulatory requirements in certain circumstances, and usually with specific conditions attached.

Table A: Exemptions

1. Buildings required for the purpose of any educational establishment erected to plans which have been approved by the Secretary of State for DES (except for houses).
2. Buildings of statutory undertakers held and used for the purpose of their undertaking.
3. Buildings subject to the Explosive Acts 1875 and 1923 and the Health and Safety at Work Etc. Act 1974.
4. Buildings (except dwellings, offices and canteens) on a site with a licence under the Nuclear Installations Act 1965.
5. Buildings subject to the Ancient Monuments and Archeological Areas Act 1979.
6. Buildings (except dwellings, offices and showrooms) used in connection with any mine or quarry.
7. Buildings into which people cannot or do not normally go.
8. Detached buildings containing fixed plant or machinery which are visited intermittently.
9. Greenhouses (unless used for retailing, packing or exhibiting).
10. Buildings used for agriculture and fish farming sited one and a half times their height from any building containing sleeping accommodation and having no point more than 30 metres from an exit which may be used in the case of fire (unless the main purpose of the building is retailing, packing or exhibiting).
11. Buildings intended to remain erected for less than 28 days.
12. Mobile homes subject to the Mobile Homes Act 1983.
13. Buildings on an estate used in connection with the sale of building or building plots provided there is no sleeping accommodation.
14. Buildings used by people in connection with the erection, extension, alteration or repair of buildings and containing no sleeping accommodation.
15. Detached buildings not exceeding 30 square metres floor area containing no sleeping accommodation and either sited more than one metre from the boundary of its curtilage or a single storey constructed of non-combustible materials.
16. Nuclear, chemical or conventional weapon shelters not exceeding 30 square metres and which do not affect the foundations of adjoining buildings.
17. Greenhouse, conversatory, porch, covered way or carport open on at least two sides which have a floor area not exceeding 30 square metres and subject to the glazing requirements of Approved Document N.
18. Certain temporary exhibition stands.
19. Tents or marquees.
20. Moveable dwellings under Section 269 of the Public Health Act 1936.
21. 'Static' mobile accommodation (e.g. caravan).
22. Certain engineering structures (e.g. dock, tunnel).
23. Tower masts not attached to buildings (not chimneys).
24. Plant or machinery.
25. Storage racking (unless supporting a floor).
26. Amusement or fairground equipment.
27. Scaffolding or falsework.
28. Street furniture.
29. Fences, walls or gates.
30. External storage tanks (not septic tanks).
31. Prison buildings: Prisons Act 1952.

Notice of Intention

It is an offence if an application by way of 2 clear days' notice is not made, but work may begin before approval is obtained.

Notification checklist

Notification to the planning authority may be in the format of:

1 FULL PLANS (in duplicate).
These should include:
- relevant form (see page 46)
- the fee (unless disabled exemption is claimed)
- drawings:
  - BLOCK PLAN (not less than 1/1250 scale) showing size and position of the building and relationship to adjoining buildings, boundaries and size, use and position of all buildings within the curtilage, width of adjoining streets, lines of drainage, size, depth and gradient of drains and means of access and ventilation, position and level of drain outfall, sewer connection and position.
  - PLANS AND SECTIONS (usually not less than 1/100) showing precise location of boundaries in relation to proposal, levels of the site of the building and lowest floor level in relation to adjoining streets, number of storeys, position, dimensions and form of foundations, walls, floors, windows, chimneys and roof, details of DPC and moisture barriers, use of all rooms and details of fire protection, means of escape in case of fire, sound and heat insulation, ventilation and access facilities for disabled people. Details of cavity fill insulation and unvented hot water systems.

2 BUILDING NOTICE
This should include:
- relevant form (see page 46)
- drawings:
  - BLOCK PLAN (not less than 1/1250 scale) showing size and position of the building and relationship to adjoining buildings, boundaries and size, use and position of all buildings within the curtilage, width of adjoining streets. Particulars of the number of storeys, use of the building, means of drainage, provision of exits, building over a public sewer, satisfying local enactments, cavity fill insulation, unvented hot water systems.

- THE BUILDING NOTICE FEE is the combined plan and inspection fees and is payable on demand after inspection by the local authority.

The local authority has no power to approve or reject a Building Notice.

3 INITIAL NOTICE (by approved inspector)
This should include:
- RELEVANT FORM (see page 46)
  Initial notice
  Combined initial notice and plans certificate
  Plans certificate
- GROUNDS
  The approved inspector must satisfy the local authority on these grounds:
  - form of the notice;
  - work is within local authority's area;
  - the person who has signed the notice is an approved inspector;
  - location and details of work;
  - approval of inspector status has been granted by a designated body;
  - insurance cover;
  - the fire authority has been consulted where required;
  - no professional or financial interest;
  - satisfactory drainage outfall;
  - building over a public sewer;
  - complying with local enactments;
  - no overlap with earlier Building Notice.

The local authority has 5 days to accept or reject the notice. If not rejected, it is presumed to have been accepted.

Time for decision

The authority should make a decision within 5 weeks unless the parties both agree to extend the period to 2 months from the date of the depositing of the plans. If the authority fails to make a decision during this period, it has breached its duty and must refund the fee, although there is no deemed approval. Rejection of an initial notice on the prescribed grounds must be made within 10 working days of its deposit.

Commencement

If the proposals are compliant, work should normally begin within 3 years of notification by the local authority, although progress rates are not specified, and work can continue indefinitely.

Notices

Local authorities require notice in writing at various stages in the construction process, although they may agree to inspection requests by other means (e.g. telephone call). Notice is required.
- 2 days before commencement
- 1 day before excavation covered
- 1 day before foundation covered
- 1 day before DPC covered
- 1 day before site concrete covered
- 1 day before drainage or sewer covered
- within 5 days of covering of drain or sewer
- 5 days before occupation if occupied before completion
- within 5 days of completion

The local authority must issue a completion certificate:
- if requested at the time of full plans submission;
- if notice has been received that the building will be put to a 'designated use';
- if notice has been received in respect of completion or part occupation before completion.

If there is an approved inspector, a final certificate must be issued when the work is complete. The local authority have 10 days in which to reject it, otherwise they are deemed to have accepted it.

BUILDING INSPECTION REQUEST

Please telephone or return this card to advise your council when the work is ready to be inspected for each stage of the works. Note all notices other than the commencement may be given by telephone

> Building Regulations
> Plan Number

Details of work

Location of site:

Builder's name and address:

Tel:

Signature: Date for inspection:

Stage of work *please tick appropriate box*   Notice required

☐ Commencement .... 2 days prior to commencement
☐ Excavation for foundations .... 1 day prior to inspection
☐ Concrete foundations .... 1 day prior to inspection
☐ Material laid on site .... 1 day prior to inspection
☐ Damp proof course laid .... 1 day prior to inspection
☐ Drain ready for inspection and test .... 1 day prior to inspection
☐ Drain backfilled and ready for test .... Within 5 days
☐ Occupation of the building (or part) .... 5 days prior to occupation
☐ Final completion .... Within 5 days

Office use only

Date of receipt: Date of inspection:

Inspected by:

Failure to inform the council may mean you will be required to uncover or remove work and could result in a fine
'Day' means any period of 24 hours commencing at midnight and excludes any Saturday, Sunday, Bank or Public holiday.

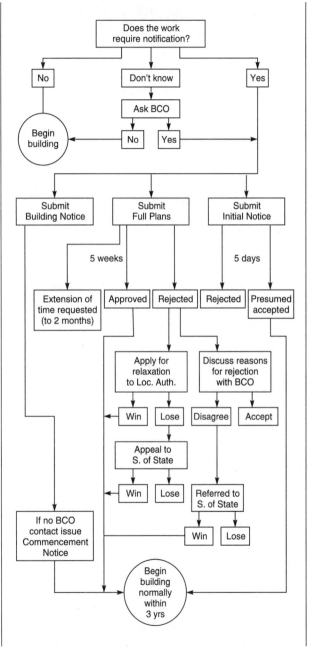

Conditional approvals

These may be granted subject to the later approval of certain details (which will be listed), for which insufficient information has been submitted to enable them to be determined as complying with the Building Regulations. A time period is not stipulated for the submission of information, but it is normal for such information to be deposited before the relevant work commences on site.

Appeals

Rejection of plans

If the notifying party feels that the local authority is wrong, the matter may be referred to the Secretary of State for determination. A fee is payable for this procedure.

Offences

It is an offence to:

- commence building without first making a proper written application to the local authority;
- fail to submit the appropriate notices;
- build contrary to the Building Regulations and Building Act 1984;
- fail to submit, in due time, details pertaining to conditional approvals.

The local authority may initiate criminal proceedings, and heavy fines usually result with a continuing liability for each day the contravention remains uncorrected. Notice to alter or remove the offending work may not be given after the expiration of 12 months from the date of completion of the work in question, except by an injunction of the High Court.

References

BUILDING REGULATIONS EXPLAINED: pp. 37, 45.

Plan checklist 1

Building Regulations 2001

Regulations

1. Title, commencement and application
2. Interpretation
3. Meaning of building work
4. Requirements relating to building work
5. Meaning of material change of use
6. Requirements relating to material change of use
7. Materials and workmanship
8. Limitation on requirements
9. Exempt buildings and work
10. Power to dispense with or relax requirements
11. Giving of a building notice or deposit of plans
12. Particulars and plans where a building notice is given
13. Full plans
14. Notice of commencement and completion of certain stages of work
15. Completion Certificate
16. Testing of drains and private sewers
17. Sampling of material
18. Local authority powers relating to partly completed work
19. Revocations
20. Transitional provisions

Plan checklist 2

PART		REQUIREMENTS
A STRUCTURE	1/2	Loading and ground movement
	3/4	Disproportionate collapse
B FIRE SAFETY	1	Means of escape
	2	Internal fire spread – linings
	3	Internal fire spread – structure
	4	External fire spread
	5	Access and facilities for the fire service
C SITE PREPARATION AND RESISTANCE TO MOISTURE	1	Preparation of site
	2	Dangerous and offensive substances
	3	Subsoil drainage
	4	Resistance to weather and ground moisture
D TOXIC SUBSTANCES	1	Cavity insulation
E AIRBORNE AND IMPACT SOUND	1	Airborne sound (walls)
	2	Airborne sound (floors and stairs)
	3	Impact sound (floors and stairs)
F VENTILATION	1	Means of ventilation
	2	Condensation
G HYGIENE	1	Sanitary conveniences and washing facilities
	2	Bathrooms
	3	Hot water storage
H DRAINAGE AND WASTE DISPOSAL	1	Foul water drainage
	2	Waste water treatment systems and cesspools
	3	Rainwater drainage
	4	Building over sewers
	5	Separate systems of drainage
	6	Solid waste storage
J COMBUSTION APPLIANCES AND FUEL STORAGE SYSTEMS	1	Air supply
	2	Discharge of products of combustion
	3	Protection of building
	4	Provision of information
	5	Protection of liquid fuel storage systems
	6	Protection against pollution

Plan checklist 3

PART		REQUIREMENTS
K PROTECTION FROM FALLING COLLISION IMPACT	1	Stairs, ladders and ramps
	2	Protection from falling
	3	Vehicle barriers and loading bays
	4	Protection from collision
	5	Trapping by doors
L CONSERVATION OF FUEL AND POWER	1	Conservation of fuel and power in dwellings
	2	Conservation of fuel and power in buildings other than dwellings
M ACCESS AND FACILITIES FOR DISABLED PEOPLE	1	Means of access to buildings
	2	Means of access in buildings
	3	Use of buildings
	4	Sanitary conveniences
	5	Audience and spectator seating
	6	Means of access: dwellings
	7	Circulation in entrance storey
	8	Accessible switches
	9	Lifts and stairs in blocks of flats
	10	WC provision: dwellings
N GLAZING – MATERIALS AND PROTECTION	1	Impact
	2	Protection against collision
	3	Opening and closing
	4	Safe cleaning

ALLIED MATTERS
Building Act 1984

Section	18	Building over a public sewer
Section	21	Satisfactory foul and storm drainage
Section	24	Exits to certain buildings
Section	25	Provisions of water supply

RELATED MATTERS
Demolition of buildings
Dangerous buildings and structures
Means of escape from fire in houses in multiple occupation
Safety at Sports Grounds
Licensing of buildings
House improvement grants

Building Notice

BUILDING ACT 1984

BUILDING REGULATIONS

BUILDING NOTICE

This notice is given in relation to the under-mentioned building work, and is submitted in accordance with Regulations 11(1)(a)

Signed ....

Date ....

FOR COUNCIL USE ONLY

NOTE: The building notice procedure cannot be used if the work is related to a building or part of a building used or intended to be used as an office or shop. For this, the FULL PLAN PROCEDURE should be used.

NAME AND ADDRESS OF PERSON ON WHOSE BEHALF THE WORK IS TO BE CARRIED OUT.

(USE CAPITAL LETTERS) POST CODE

DESCRIPTION OF PROPOSED WORK

IF SIGNED BY AGENT, NAME AND ADDRESS OF AGENT.
TEL
(USE CAPITAL LETTERS) POST CODE

NUMBER OF STOREYS ....

ADDRESS AT WHICH THE WORK IS TO BE CARRIED OUT.

(USE CAPITAL LETTERS)

ESTIMATED COST WHERE APPLICABLE
£ ....
(SEE SEPARATE FEE SHEET)

FEE

V.A.T.

TOTAL

REFER TO SEPARATE FEE SHEET FOR FEE DUE.

DO **NOT** SEND FEE WITH THIS NOTICE, THE PERSON HAVING THE WORK CARRIED OUT WILL BE INVOICED WHEN WORK COMMENCES.

SEND ONE COPY OF THIS NOTICE, ALONG WITH PLANS AND DETAILS MENTIONED OVERLEAF.

WHERE THE WORK IS, OR INVOLVES THE INSERTION OF INSULATING MATERIAL IN EXISTING CAVITY WALLS

MATERIAL

BBA/BSI CERTIFICATE NO.

INSTALLER

WHERE THE WORK IS, OR INVOLVES THE INSTALLATION OF AN UNVENTED HOT WATER SYSTEM

SYSTEM

BBA CERTIFICATE NO.

INSTALLER

NOTE: A SEPARATE NOTICE OF COMMENCEMENT MUST BE GIVEN IN WRITING NOT LESS THAN 48 HOURS BEFORE WORK STARTS.

Building Notice

Final Certificate

FINAL CERTIFICATE

1. This certificate relates to the following work:

2. I am an approved inspector and the work described above was [the whole]/[part] of the work described in an initial notice given by me and dated

3. Subject to what is said in paragraph 4 below, the work described above has been completed and I have performed the functions assigned to me by regulation 10 of the 1985 regulations.

4. The work described above involves the insertion of insulating material into a cavity wall and this [has]/[has not] been carried out

5. The work described above does not include, so far as I am aware, the erection of any building or extension over a sewer shown on the relative map of sewers, except—

(a) work about which information was given with the initial notice, or

(b) work about which I notified the local authority on in accordance with my obligation under regulation 10 of the 1985 regulations.

6. Final certificates have now been issued in respect of all the work described in the initial notice referred to in paragraph 2 above.

7. With this certificate is a declaration signed by the insurer that a named scheme of insurance approved by the Secretary of State applies in relation to the work to which the certificate relates.

8. The work [is]/[is not] minor work

9. I have had no professional or financial interest in the work described above since giving the initial notice described in paragraph 2 above.

10. I have consulted the fire authority in accordance with regulation 11 of the 1985 regulations

Signed

Date Approved Inspector.

Final Certificate

Full Plans Submission

FULL PLANS SUBMISSION

APPLICATION IS MADE FOR APPROVAL UNDER BUILDING REGULATIONS: this application is being made under regulation 11(1)(b)

Signed Dated

APPLICANT (in block letters) TEL. No.

Name

Address

Post Code

AGENT (if any) (in block letters)

Name

Address

Daytime Tel. No. Post Code

DESCRIPTION OF PROPOSED BUILDING WORK

LOCATION OR ADDRESS OF PROPOSED BUILDING WORK

What are the existing and proposed uses of the Building or affected part(s)?

FOR COUNCIL USE ONLY

PLAN NUMBER

DATE RECEIVED

Have there been any previous Building Regulations Applications submitted for the project? YES/NO

If YES, Plan No.

Has Planning Permission Plan No.
been granted? YES/NO

PLEASE COMPLETE APPROPRIATE SECTION OVERLEAF REGARDING FEES

SUBMISSION OF PLANS

1. This application is for the Building Regulations only. A separate application must be made if necessary under the TOWN AND COUNTRY PLANNING ACTS or any other legislation.

2. TWO APPLICATION FORMS AND TWO COPIES OF ALL PLANS MUST BE SUBMITTED. (For those applications where calculations are required you are advised to submit an additional copy of the plan; this will expedite the decision.)

3. The plans must include:
   (1) Block plan - not less than 1/1250
   (2) Foundation, floor and roof plans - not less than 1/100
   (3) Elevations - not less than 1/100
   (4) Sections - not less than 1/100
   (5) Details as necessary
   (6) Calculations as necessary (e.g. structural, thermal insulation etc.)

Full Plans Submission

Plans Certificate

PLANS CERTIFICATE

1. This certificate relates to the following work:

2. I am an approved inspector for the purposes of Part II of the Act and the above work is [the whole]/[part] of the work described in an initial notice given by me and dated

3. With this certificate is the declaration, signed by the insurer, that a named scheme of insurance approved by the Secretary of State applies in relation to the work to which the certificate relates.

4. Plans of the work specified above have been submitted to me and I am satisfied that the plans neither are defective nor show that work carried out in accordance with them would contravene any provision of building regulations.

5. The work [is]/[is not] minor work.

6. I declare that I have had no financial or professional interest in the work described since giving the initial notice described in paragraph 2.

7. I have consulted the fire authority in accordance with regulation 11.

8. The plans to which this certificate relates bear the following date and reference number:

Date

Signed
Approved Inspector

Plans Certificate

Combined Initial Notice and Plans Certificate

COMBINED INITIAL NOTICE AND PLANS CERTIFICATE

To

1. This notice relates to the following work:

2. The approved inspector in relation to the work is:

3. The person intending to carry out the work is:

4. With this notice are the following documents, which are those relevant to the work described in this notice

(a) in the case of a notice signed by an inspector approved by a designated body in accordance with regulation 3(2) of the 1985 regulations, a copy of the notice of his approval

(b) a declaration signed by the insurer that a named scheme of insurance approved by the Secretary of State applies in relation to the work described in the notice.

(c) in the case of the erection or extension of a building, a plan to a scale of not less than 1:1250 showing the boundaries and location of the site and a statement—

(i) as to the approximate location of any proposed connection to be made to a sewer, or

(ii) if no connection is to be made to a sewer, as to the proposals for the discharge of any proposed drain, including the location of any cesspool, or

(iii) if no provision is to be made for drainage, of the reasons why none is necessary.

(d) where it is proposed to erect a building or extension over a sewer or drain shown on the relative map of sewers, a statement as to the location of the building or extension and the precautions to be taken in building over the sewer or drain

(e) a statement of any local enactment relevant to the work, and of the steps to be taken to comply with it

5. The work [is]/[is not] minor work

6. I declare that I do not, and will not while this notice is in force, have any financial or professional interest in the work described

7. I am satisfied that plans relating to the work described above have been submitted to me, and that they neither are defective nor show work which, if carried out in accordance with them, would contravene any provision of building regulations.

8. The approved inspector [is]/[is not] obliged to consult the fire authority by regulation 11 of the 1985 regulations.

9. I have consulted the fire authority in accordance with regulation 11

10. I undertake to consult the fire authority before giving a final certificate in accordance with section 51 of the Act in respect of any of the work described above.

11. The plans to which this certificate relates bear the following date and reference number:

12. I am aware of the obligations laid upon me by Part II of the Act and by regulation 10 of the 1985 regulations.

Signed Signed

Approved Inspector Date Person intending to Date
carry out the work.

Combined Initial Notice and Plans Certificate

Initial Notice

The Building (Approved Inspectors etc.) Regulations 1985 ("the 1985 regulations")

INITIAL NOTICE

To

1. This notice relates to the following work:

2. The approved inspector in relation to the work is:

3. The person intending to carry out the work is:

4. With this notice are the following documents, which are those relevant to the work described in this notice

(a) in the case of a notice signed by an inspector approved by a designated body in accordance with regulation 3(2) of the 1985 regulations, a copy of the notice of his approval

(b) a declaration signed by the insurer that a named scheme of insurance approved by the Secretary of State applies in relation to the work described in the notice.

(c) in the case of the erection or extension of a building, a plan to a scale of not less than 1:1250 showing the boundaries and location of the site and a statement—

(i) as to the approximate location of any proposed connection to be made to a sewer, or

(ii) if no connection is to be made to a sewer, as to the proposals for the discharge of any proposed drain, including the location of any cesspool, or

(iii) if no provision is to be made for drainage, of the reasons why none is necessary

(d) where it is proposed to erect a building or extension over a sewer or drain shown on the relative map of sewers, a statement as to the location of the building or extension and the precautions to be taken in building over the sewer or drain

(e) a statement of any local enactment relevant to the work, and of the steps to be taken to comply with it

5. The work [is]/[is not] minor work

6. I declare that I do not, and will not while this notice is in force, have any financial or professional interest in the work described.

7. The approved inspector [will]/[will not] be obliged to consult the fire authority by regulation 11 of the 1985 regulations

8. I undertake to consult the fire authority before giving a plans certificate in accordance with section 50 of the Act or a final certificate in accordance with section 51 of the Act in respect of any of the work described above

9. I am aware of the obligations laid upon me by Part II of the Act and by regulation 10 of the 1985 regulations

Signed Signed

Approved Inspector Date Person intending to Date
carry out the work

Initial Notice

C. Outline Proposals

At this stage it is necessary to approximate the potential cost of the proposed scheme, and to produce an outline cost plan. Although this is normally the province of the quantity surveyor, smaller jobs may be handled by the architect without assistance.

Methods of approximate estimation include:

- COST PER SQUARE METRE BASIS: fairly common and easy to calculate;
- COST PER CUBE BASIS: useful because it takes into account roof heights and non-standard spaces;
- COST PER UNIT RATE: where a price is determined at £x per individual placing or per room etc. This method can be useful when dealing with schools or similar institutions;
- COST PER ITEM: this is more useful where difficult work such as renovations would need to be broken down into measurable elements, and individually priced.

D. Detailed Proposals

E. Final Proposals

The specification

- forms part of the Standard Form 'Private without Quantities';
- does not form part of the Standard Form 'Private with Quantities', although a specification is usually included as part of the Bills of Quantities;
- forms part of the contract as well as the Bills of Quantities in Standard Form GC/Works/1 and certain other public authority contracts.

The specification should be read with the drawings and other schedules. It sets out the precise quality and sometimes the quantities of the materials to be used, and the standard of the workmanship required. Preliminary clauses cover definitions of procedure, responsibilities and general outline of the work. The remaining clauses are usually based on the Common Arrangement of Work Sections for building works (CAWS).

National Building Specification

The National Building Specification is a directory of clauses covering materials, workmanship and their quality, and these clauses are intended to adapt to each particular project, obviating the need to rewrite the specification every time. It fully complies with the Co-ordinated Project Information Code of Procedure for Project Specifications. It is now available on CD-ROM.

F. Product Information

Consideration of tender action begins at this stage (see page 60).

G. Tender Documentation

Although often prepared trade by trade, it is now more usual for them to be prepared following the Standard Method of Measurement (SMM 7) arranged in the following categories:

A Preliminaries/General conditions
C Demolition/Alteration/Renovation
D Groundwork
E In situ concrete/Large precast concrete
F Masonry
G Structural/Carcassing metal/Timber
H Cladding/Covering
J Waterproofing
K Linings/Sheathing/Dry partitioning
L Windows/Doors/Stairs
M Surface finishes
N Furniture/Equipment
P Building fabric sundries
Q Paving/Planting/Fencing/Site furniture
R Disposal systems
S Piped supply systems
T Mechanical heating/Cooling/Refrigeration systems
U Ventilation/Air conditioning systems
V Electrical supply/Power/Lighting systems
W Communications/Security/Control systems
X Transport systems
Y Mechanical and electrical services measurement

Working drawings tips

Although there is widespread use of computers to prepare drawings, many practices still practise traditional drawing by hand.

- Estimate number of drawings necessary, to facilitate office programming.
- Draw only as much as is necessary. Time and money are often wasted duplicating data which is adequately covered elsewhere (e.g. in the specification).
- Can time be saved in the drawing process? A base drawing may be used to add 'layers' of information onto a duplicated original.
- Decide on a standard method of cross reference throughout the job.
- Organise drawings into:
  - KEY DRAWINGS
  - ASSEMBLY DRAWINGS
  - COMPONENT DRAWINGS
  - SCHEDULES

BS 1192: Construction Drawing Practice should be consulted for a fuller guide to working drawings.

- Make sure every sheet contains (if applicable)
  - PROJECT TITLE
  - SHEET TITLE
  - DRAUGHTER
  - NORTH POINT
  - DATE
  - DRAWING NUMBER
  - REVISION SPACE
  - CHECKED BY
  - SCALES
- Build up a collection of A4 standard details that are likely to be useful on future projects.

References

THE ARCHITECT IN PRACTICE, pp. 168–235.
ARCHITECT'S HANDBOOK OF PRACTICE MANAGEMENT, pp. 186–93.

MEMO

To : Tom Square
From : D. Taylor
Date : 17. May
Concerning : Building Regs. re. Careful's Job.

MR. CAREFUL phoned & wants bldg to start soon. Told him we had planning permission & a builder lined up, but hadn't heard from bldg control yet. He said how can we speed them up. I said you'd be in touch.
Dave.

LOCKE, STOCKE and BARRELL

SOLICITORS

...cke.LLB(Lond).
...cke.MA(Oxon).
...rell.BA(Rangoon).

...BB/bg

1, Fore ...
Cringing,
Wilts.

WITHOUT PREJUDICE

14.5.02

Dear Sirs,

re: New development in Cheapsgate, Cringing

We have been instructed by Mr Vic Sassious, whose property abuts that of your client, Mr B. Careful.

We are informed that various materials have been dumped on our client's property, and that a large stock of bricks has been left in such a way as to block the gateway. Furthermore, our client fears for the safety of his children, who may be in danger of injuring themselves as a result of your client's excavations.

Although our client is considering taking legal action, we are instructed that he is prepared to settle the matter for immediate compensation of £1,500.

We look forward to hearing from you.

Yours faithfully,

Locke, Stocke & Barrell
Locke, Stocke and Barrell

Messrs. F...
4, The He...
Cringing,
Wilts.

South Cringing Rural Action Group

27.5.02

To: Messrs Fair and Square.

Sirs,

As President of SCRAG, I am writing to you to inform you of the deep concern expressed by our members about your proposals for a new Day Centre in Cringing. We feel that the uncompromisingly modern approach you have taken is not in keeping with the present surroundings, and will be detrimental to the area as a whole.

Accordingly, we must insist that you reconsider your plans and try and come up with something more in keeping with the existing buildings.

Should you persist in your present endeavours, we will be forced to take the matter to the Secretary of State and our local Member Mr. Gavin Gracefully.

...urs sincerely,

ANN THROP (Miss)

DESK DIARY

MAY 27

re: bldg regs/Careful.
Tell Dave permission isn't necessary,
just notification (although the work must
conform to the regs). We could go ahead,
but I'd rather contact the authorities first -
they provide a useful check on our work.

MAY 28

re: SCRAG.
Better Acknowledge receipt of letter and
warn clients - then wait and see what
happens. A meeting with SCRAG may be
useful later on to explain the scheme.
Uncompromisingly modern ?!!

MAY 29

Vicki - send this
off to SCRAG
please.
Tom

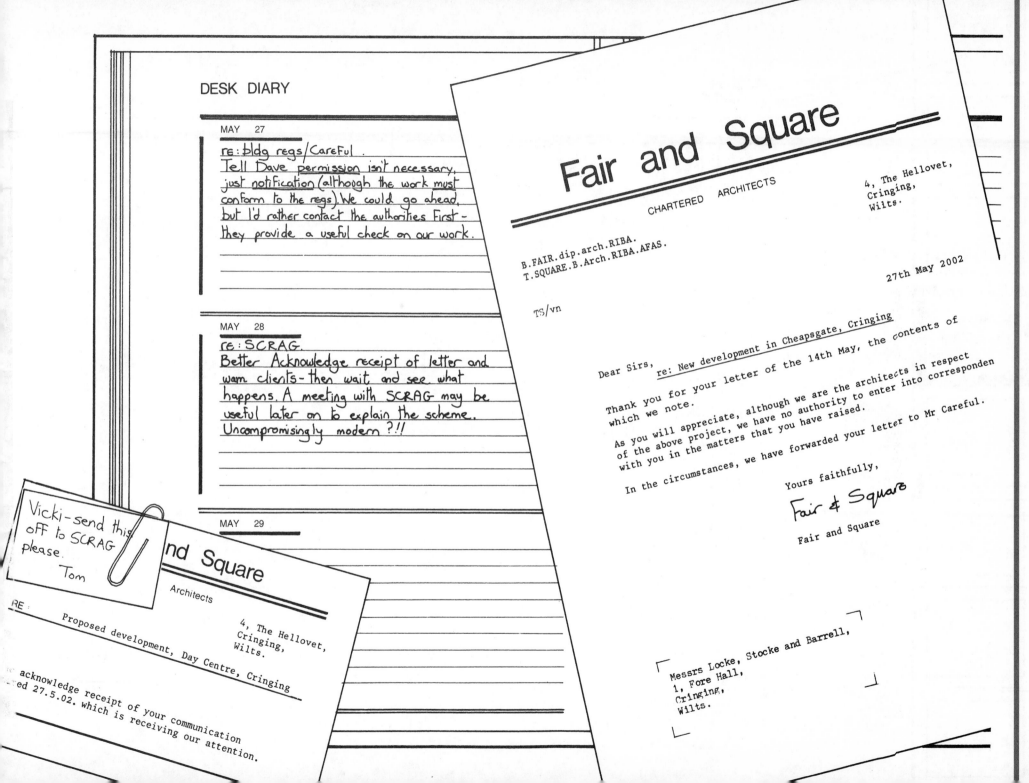

Fair and Square

CHARTERED ARCHITECTS

4, The Hellovet,
Cringing,
Wilts.

B.FAIR.dip.arch.RIBA.
T.SQUARE.B.Arch.RIBA.AFAS.

27th May 2002

TS/vn

Dear Sirs, re: New development in Cheapsgate, Cringing

Thank you for your letter of the 14th May, the contents of
which we note.

As you will appreciate, although we are the architects in respect
of the above project, we have no authority to enter into corresponden
with you in the matters that you have raised.

In the circumstances, we have forwarded your letter to Mr Careful.

Yours faithfully,

Fair & Square

Fair and Square

Messrs Locke, Stocke and Barrell,
1, Fore Hall,
Cringing,
Wilts.

nd Square

Architects

4, The Hellovet,
Cringing,
Wilts.

RE : Proposed development, Day Centre, Cringing

acknowledge receipt of your communication
ed 27.5.02. which is receiving our attention.

49

CONTRACT FORMATION

Contents

RIBA
**Work Stage
H**

The contract

A contract has been defined as:

> A legally binding agreement between two or more parties, by which rights are acquired by one or more to acts or forebearances on the part of the other or others.
>
> *Sir William Anson*

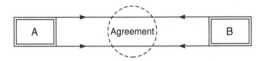

Formation

Contracts may be formed in a number of ways:

a ORALLY

A contractual relationship may be formed between parties in some cases where no written agreement exists, but an oral contract was made.

b BY CONDUCT

The actions of parties may be such as to prove a contractual relationship between them.

c BY DEED

Some contracts must be formed by deed. These include leases of land for more than 3 years, transfers of titles to land and contracts where there is no valuable consideration.

d IN WRITING

Certain kinds of contracts must be formed in writing if they are to be enforceable. These include hire purchase agreements and assignments of copyright.

e EVIDENCED IN WRITING

Other contracts, for example contracts of guarantee and contracts for the sale of land, need to be evidenced in writing if they are to be enforceable.

Validity

Contracts may be:

- valid;
- void, without any legal effect;
- voidable, i.e. valid until one of the parties repudiates;
- unenforceable in the courts.

Elements

The contractual agreement involves certain rights and obligations for the parties concerned, which may be enforceable in law. However, there are a number of basic elements which are necessary for the creation of a legally binding and enforceable contract:

1 OFFER AND ACCEPTANCE

An offer by one party must be clearly made, and that offer must be unconditionally accepted by the other party. Upon acceptance, the contract comes into effect.

2 INTENTION

This must be shown by both parties, indicating their desire to enter into a legally binding contract.

3 CAPACITY

All parties to the contract must have a legal capacity to do so. For example, minors, persons of unsound mind, corporations, etc. may be excluded from certain types of contract.

4 CONSENT

Consent must be proper, and not obtained from either party by fraud or duress.

5 LEGALITY

The contract must be formed within the boundaries of the law. For example, a contract to commit a crime would not be binding.

6 POSSIBILITY

Contracts formed to undertake impossible tasks are unenforceable.

7 CONSIDERATION

Each party must contribute something in consideration of the other's promise. This must be:

- REAL
- NOT NECESSARILY ADEQUATE
- LEGAL
- POSSIBLE
- NOT IN THE PAST
- AND MUST MOVE FROM THE PROMISE

Privity

Privity is a legal doctrine which recognises that only a party to a contract may sue upon it. There are certain limited exceptions to this general rule, e.g. where an agency relationship exists, the principal is bound by contracts entered into by his or her agent with third parties. This doctrine was reviewed *Contracts for the Benefit of Third Parties*, HMSO Law Commission Consultation Paper 121, 1991. As a result, the Contracts (Rights of Third Parties) Act 1999 was passed by Parliament (see page 9).

Discharge

Once a contract has been formed, it can be discharged in a number of ways:

- PERFORMANCE
  By realisation of the agreement within the terms of the contract.
- AGREEMENT
  Agreement by both parties to cease their contractual relationship.
- OPERATION OF LAW
  For example, if a contract is formed for a limited period, and that period expires.
- FRUSTRATION OR SUBSEQUENT IMPOSSIBILITY
  Performance of the contract may be possible at the outset, but be later frustrated by events (e.g. death of a party, destruction of an element constituting the basis of the contract.

Breach

A breach occurs when either party to the contract does not fulfil their obligations. If the breach 'goes to the root' of the contract, it is treated as discharged, and the injured party may seek one of the following remedies:

1 REFUSAL OF FURTHER PERFORMANCE

Refusal to continue with their part of the contract.

2 RESCISSION

This is a discretionary remedy, enabling the courts to cancel or annul the contract.

3 AN ACTION FOR SPECIFIC PERFORMANCE

The party in breach is ordered to fulfil their obligations within the contract.

4 AN ACTION FOR AN INJUNCTION

A legal measure taken to prevent further actions by the party in breach.

5 AN ACTION FOR DAMAGES

Damages for breach of contract could be:

- general, that is arising out of the breach;
- special, for example, loss of earnings;
- nominal, if the breach is only technical;
- contemptuous, where the court, by the level of damages awarded, expresses its contempt of the action brought;
- exemplary, which would be partly punitive;
- liquidated damages (see page 80);
- unliquidated damages (unascertained).

6 AN ACTION FOR A 'QUANTUM MERUIT'

A claim for a sum for 'as much as he has earned'.

Building Contracts

Types of contract

A building contract may take any form which is agreeable to the parties involved, but certain proven methods of contracting have been developed which are useful in differing building situations. These include:
- lump sum contracts
- measurement contracts
- cost reimbursement contracts

Lump sum

The contractor agrees in advance to undertake a specified amount of work for a fixed price. The inflexible nature of the price may mean that the contractor could fall foul of inflation or unforeseen circumstances, and may be inclined to raise prices as a safeguard. There are two forms of lump sum contract:
1 LUMP SUM WITH PLAN AND SPECIFICATION, which is used for minor building projects and repair work where the requirements are simple and easily definable.
2 LUMP SUM WITH BILLS OF QUANTITIES, which is used in most building work of a traditional nature.
In practice, variation, fluctuation and loss and/or expense clauses relieve the contractor of some of the consequences.

Measurement

A price for the work is determined by measurement and valuation in relation to agreed price formulas and rates. A measurement contract may be based on:
1 APPROXIMATE QUANTITIES, where, on completion of the work, the contractor is paid according to the prices established in an approximate bill of quantities. This method is useful when the employer's requirements are unsure in the earlier stages of the project, as it allows competitive tendering to be used and gives a reasonable idea of what the final cost may be.
2 A SCHEDULE, where the outcome of the work is so vague as to preclude even an approximate set of quantities. Instead, the work is carried out and measured according to an agreed schedule of prices. This method is suitable for minor works, repairs, etc.

Cost reimbursement

The contractor is paid the actual cost of the work, plus an agreed price to cover overheads and afford a profit. Methods of using this type of contract include:
1 COST PLUS FIXED FEE, a method sometimes employed where a rough estimate of the final cost can be made.
2 COST PLUS PERCENTAGE, where the percentage is calculated on the final cost of the work. This method is suitable for experimental projects and complex renovations, for example. Its main disadvantage is that it provides no incentive to the contractor to work quickly or to keep the costs down.
3 COST PLUS FLUCTUATING FEE, where the fee varies in an inverse ratio to whether the ultimate cost is more or less than an estimate agreed at the outset. This is a useful arrangement, as it encourages economy and speed, but demands work involving a cost prediction.
4 TARGET COST. The contractor is paid either all costs and an additional fee agreed upon earlier, or the value of the completed work based upon a schedule of prices, depending upon which is less. This method requires measurement, valuation and cost accounting.
5 VALUE COST. The contractor receives a variable fee assessed in terms of a percentage of a valuation based on a schedule of prices. Should the final cost be actually lower or higher, the fee fluctuates accordingly. This method tends to be used by larger organisations which have suitable facilities for valuation and general accounting.

Overseas contracts

British architects are becoming increasingly involved in work overseas. In these circumstances, great care should be taken at the contract formation stage to avoid difficulties which might arise in enforcing the agreement due to:
- conflict between the laws in the parties' countries;
- the contractual capacity or immunity of the parties.
Before entering into any such contracts, it is advisable to seek specialist legal advice.

Contract checklist

Some of the more important factors to be taken into consideration when considering which type of contract to suggest to the client include:
- type of project;
- size and complexity;
- time constraints;
- finance available;
- extent of the definition of the employer's requirements;
- likelihood of change in these requirements;
- amount of information available at contract formation;
- availability of accurate cost predictions;
- expertise available;
- facilities for measurement, valuation and accounting;
- external problems, e.g. the constraints on the site, labour shortages, etc;
- quality of work required (e.g. luxury or prestige work).

References

ARCHITECT'S HANDBOOK OF PRACTICE MANAGEMENT, pp. 7.
ARCHITECT'S LEGAL HANDBOOK, pp. 8–18.
LAW, pp. 97–173.

Standard forms of contract

Just as any type of contract (see page 52) can be chosen by the parties concerned, so can any form of the agreement be used to set out the terms between the parties. In 1964, the Banwell Committee found that it would be preferable to develop a standard form of contract for the entire construction industry although Latham, in his 1994 Report on the construction industry, did not support this view, but did favour the Engineering and Construction Contract (ECC). There are a number of standard forms which attempt to deal with the complexities and contingencies which may arise in the construction process.

Some employers, particularly large bodies like government departments, may insist on using their own form. For example, GC/WKS/1 which is used on government associated contracts places a heavier burden upon the contractor than is usual in private contracts. Furthermore, certain professional bodies have developed their own forms (e.g. the Institution of Civil Engineers and the Association of Consultant Architects).

Generally though, the most commonly used standard forms are published by the RIBA in conjuction with the Joint Contracts Tribunal Ltd, and should be used wherever possible. Should the employer wish to deviate from or embellish the conditions in any way, it is advisable to take legal advice on the probable effect of the changes before proceeding.

JCT forms

The major standard forms of contract produced by the JCT are:
THE STANDARD FORM OF BUILDING CONTRACT 1998:
- Private with Quantities
- Private without Quantities
- Private with Approximate Quantities
- Local Authority Edition with Quantities
- Local Authority Edition without Quantities
- Local Authority Edition with Approximate Quantities
Supplements to these include:
- Fluctuations Supplement
- Sectional Completion Supplement
- Contractor's Designed Portion Supplement

Others

Other standard forms include:
- JCT Management Contract
- JCT Standard Form of Building Contract with Contractor's Design
- JCT Agreement for Minor Building Works
- JCT Form of Prime Cost Contract
- Building Contract and Scottish Supplement to the JCT Conditions of Contract
- ICE Form (for Civil Engineering Work)
- ASI Short Form of Contract
- ACA Form of Building Agreement
- NEC Contract

'Private with Quantities'

The Standard Form of Building Contract – Private with Quantities (1998 Edition) is one of the most frequently used, and will be examined in more detail in the following pages.

The form consists of:
- the Articles of Agreement (see page 54), indicating names and details of the agreement;
- the Conditions (see page 54), determining the procedures and conduct of the parties;
- the Appendix, containing dates, amounts, rates, etc.

References

ARCHITECT'S LEGAL HANDBOOK, pp. 59–172.
JCT STANDARD FORM OF BUILDING CONTRACT, 1998 EDITION, PRIVATE WITH QUANTITIES.

Dated _____

Standard Form of Building Contract
1998 Edition
Private With Quantities

Articles of Agreement and Conditions of Building Contract

between _____

_____

_____

and _____

_____

_____

Issued by The Joint Contracts Tribunal Limited

Members
Association of Consulting Engineers
British Property Federation
Construction Confederation
Local Government Association
National Specialist Contractors Council
Royal Institute of British Architects
Royal Institution of Chartered Surveyors
Scottish Building Contract Committee

The Conditions 1

Articles of agreement

Recitals

The Recitals address the following:
- Details of the works.
- Statement that the contractor has supplied the employer with a fully priced copy of the bills of quantities (or priced activity schedule).
- Reference to the drawings by number and signed by the parties.
- Status of the employer in regard to the tax deduction scheme included in Appendix.
- Extent of application of CDM Regulations stated in Appendix.
- Provision by employer to contractor of information release schedule.
- Requirement by employer of a bond on the terms agreed between the JCT and the British Bankers' Association.

Article 1

Contractor's obligation to carry out and complete the work as specified in the contract documents.

Article 2

The amount payable to the contractor by the employer, the Contract Sum.

Article 3

Identification of the architect and provision for renomination in the event of death or ceasing to act.

Article 4

Similar provisions in respect of the quantity surveyor.

Article 5

Settlement of certain differences or disputes by adjudication.

Article 6.1

Identification of planning supervisor.

Article 6.2

Principal contractor identified as contractor.

Article 7A and 7B

Options for the settlement of differences and disputes by either arbitration or legal proceedings.

The Conditions

Part One: General

1 INTERPRETATIONS, DEFINITIONS etc. of words and phrases within the contract documents.

2 CONTRACTOR'S OBLIGATIONS to carry out the work as detailed in the contract documents, and to the 'reasonable satisfaction' of the architect where approval of materials and workmanship is required.

The Contract Bills cannot override or modify the Articles, Conditions or Appendix. Errors in the Contract Bills do not vitiate the contract, and shall be corrected. The contractor must inform the architect in writing of any discrepancies in the contract documents, the numbered documents or architect's instructions that he discovers, after which the architect will give further instructions.

3 Additions, deductions or alterations to the CONTRACT SUM to be taken into account in the interim certificate following ascertainment.

4 ARCHITECT'S INSTRUCTIONS must be complied with by the contractor as long as:
1) they are made in writing;
2) they are made within the architect's powers as detailed in the contract;
3) they do not involve a variation of obligations imposed by the employer regarding access, space, hours or order of work, to which the contractor has objected in writing;
4) An instruction requiring a 13A quotation must not be carried out until the architect has accepted the quotation or an instruction is issued requiring that the work be undertaken.

The contractor may ask the architect to specify the enabling provision and seek arbitration if unsatisfied.

Non-compliance within 7 days of written notice requiring action enables the employer to have the work done and charged to the contractor (or deducted from the next payment). Unwritten instructions have no effect unless confirmed by the architect or contractor in writing within 7 days. If the contractor complies with an unwritten instruction, the architect may confirm it at any time before the issuance of the Final Certificate.

5 The architect (or quantity surveyor) retains the CONTRACT DOCUMENTS, which should be reasonably accessible to the employer or contractor. After contract formation, the contractor is entitled to a specified number of copies of the documents (see page 62) and two copies of any further information that is necessary (none of which must add obligations beyond those in the contract documents). Except to the extent that he or she is prevented by the contractor, the architect shall ensure the contractor receives two copies of the information identified in the information release schedule. In return, the architect is entitled to two copies of the contractor's master programme updated as necessary to take account of extensions of time. The contractor must keep a full set of contract drawings, descriptive schedules and the master programme on site, to be reasonably accessible to the architect at all reasonable times. All drawings should be returned at the end of the job, and all contract documents are confidential and must not be used for any purpose other than the contract. All certificates should be issued by the architect to the employer with copies to the contractor.

The contractor is to supply copies of the as-built drawings and maintenance and operating manuals before practical completion.

6 The contractor must comply with all STATUTORY REQUIREMENTS and pay all statutory fees (recoverable from the employer) in connection with the job. If any divergencies are found between these requirements and the contract documents or instructions, the architect must be notified in writing, thus absolving the contractor from liability to the employer. The architect, whether hearing of the discrepancy from the contractor or any other source, must then issue instructions within 7 days to resolve the divergence. In emergencies, the contractor may secure immediate compliance with statutory requirements prior to instructions, but must inform the architect immediately. Upon notification, the architect will treat the work as a variation using an Architect's Instruction. Contractual provisions in respect of assignment of sub-letting do not govern statutory undertakings. The employer is to ensure that the planning supervisor and principal contractor (if not the contractor) fulfil their duties under the CDM Regulations. If the contractor acts as the principal contractor, he or she must comply with the CDM Regulations.

7 The architect determines any required LEVELS and supplies adequate data to enable SETTING OUT of the works by the contractor, who is liable for errors in setting out. However,

Bird's eyeview: walking time line excercise (1)

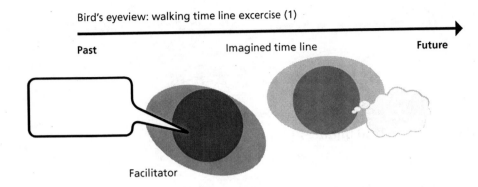

Past   Imagined time line   Future

Facilitator

5. Imagine attaching a golden thread from your goal to your navel that will draw you towards your goal and keep you on track, just like the thread that allowed Theseus to escape from the Minotaur's maze!

6. Walk forwards into your future along your time line, until you reach the place where the goal belongs. Allow the goal to gently slot into place. You may imagine hearing a click as it does so.

Bird's eyeview: walking time line excercise (2)

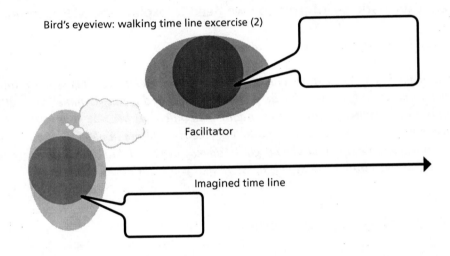

Facilitator

Imagined time line

7. Keeping your thread attached, say to the group: *I am walking back to now, only as fast as my unconscious mind can make all the adjustments needed to take me easily and effortlessly to my goal*. The facilitator will need to say these words correctly phrased for their partner when the group practise the technique, so have this on a flip chart.

i.e. Walk back to now, only as fast as your unconscious mind can make all the adjustments needed to take you easily and effortlessly to your goal.

Bird's eyeview: walking time line excercise (3)

Facilitator

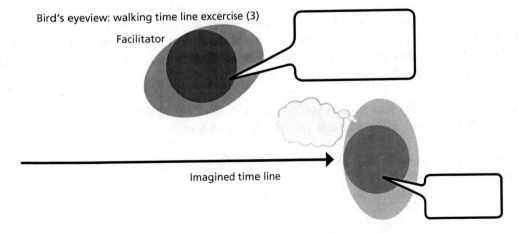

Imagined time line

1. Decide the states you are going to model for the group. Energised states are more visible as the non-verbal signals are stronger (e.g. colour change, breathing rate, etc.). Ensure that you can access these states and model them visibly for the group.

Bird's eyeview: spatial anchoring (spotlighting) 1

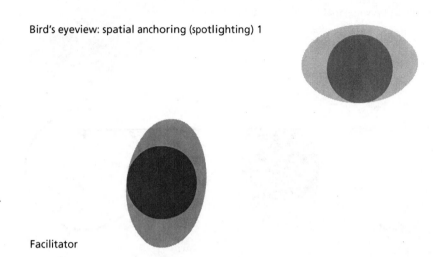

Facilitator

2. Imagine a circle on the floor. Choose the first state to go into the spotlight and tell the group what this is. Access the state, making the process visible for the group, describing a time when you felt that state strongly, using visual, auditory and kinaesthetic (VAK) descriptions, e.g. what you could *see*, *feel* (where in your body?), *hear*, etc. When the state is rising strongly, step into the circle for 10 seconds.

Bird's eyeview: spatial anchoring (spotlighting) 2

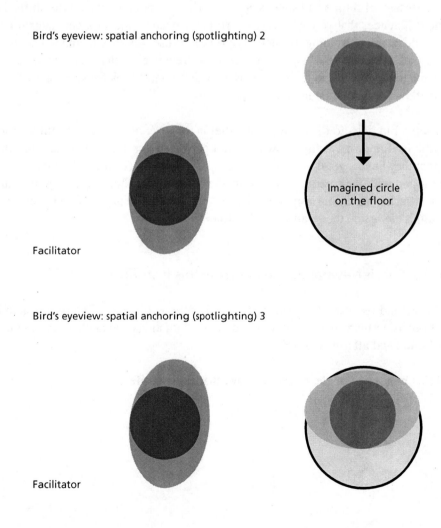

Imagined circle on the floor

Facilitator

Bird's eyeview: spatial anchoring (spotlighting) 3

Facilitator

3. Step out and imagine leaving that state in the circle. Break your state by thinking about something completely different, and now explain what you have done and the importance of this.

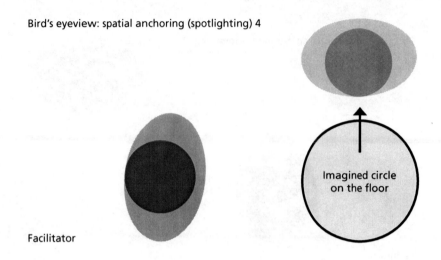

Bird's eyeview: spatial anchoring (spotlighting) 4

Imagined circle on the floor

Facilitator

4. Repeat this process for two other states, ensuring that you explicitly model how it is that you are re-creating the states strongly in yourself.

5. Break state to clear yourself completely. Now it is time to test the anchor!

6. Think of a situation when that resource would be useful (in the classroom, in meetings, etc.). Access this unresourceful time and state, step into the circle and then model the shifts that happen. Describe the differences that you are aware of. You may need to add stronger states if necessary. If you are confident about training this activity you could use someone from the audience. Make sure that you pick someone who is quite extravert and 'reactive' so that changes in their emotional state are visible to the rest of the group. This is easy to do—just look for someone who usually has noticeably different and contrasting facial expressions.

7. Send the group off in pairs to facilitate one another in this exercise. A very useful instruction here is that the facilitator may only allow the other person to step into the circle when they are convinced that they have a good, strong state. Another useful tip is for the facilitator to ensure that they are in rapport with their partner and access the desired state themselves, e.g. be enthusiastic if your partner is anchoring enthusiasm, confident if they are confident, etc. Finally, ensure that the facilitator stands alongside their partner, rather than facing them.

Part 4 (What if): Debrief—what do we get from this learning?

1. Collect reactions and feedback from the exercise. Go beyond like or dislike for the activity to what is learned about using their inner resources in different situations. What changes did they notice in themselves before and after this exercise?

2. How could this be applied in class, meetings or other areas of life?

Training exercise 5

Putting goals into your future using your time line—or 'making it happen'

(Estimated time needed: 30 minutes)

Part 1 (Why): Introduction—some possible questions to ask at the start

- Do you ever decide you want something and then find it doesn't happen, or make plans and target that you don't follow through?
- If you have decided on your goals, would it be helpful for you to have a way of making them happen?

Part 2 (What): Explanation—information we need to explain the NLP technique

Re-read Chapter 12, *You can do it ... and it's about time.*

Just as we have memories of the past, we can also create 'future memories'. These are a full represen tion of what you want, already achieved, with pictures, sounds and feelings, and even smells and tast This technique is a way of making sure that your goals and outcomes become your reality. By using yo time line, you can help your unconscious mind to have the right filters in place so that you are aware all the things that will enable you to fulfil your goal. You may even find that after doing this exercise, yo unconscious mind will generate ways of getting there that you hadn't even thought of.

Part 3 (How): Activity—set up the exercise

The best way to teach this technique is to demonstrate it yourself, with a commentary to make yo processing explicit to the group. The group can then practise it in pairs. Remember to ensure that t facilitator stands alongside their partner and is in good rapport.

1. Decide on a goal that you want for yourself. In NLP we often use a scale of 1 to 10 to grade goals we are going to deal with, where 1 represents a small goal and 10 represents a huge life change. For teaching purposes and to facilitate a positive experience it is best to use goals up to 3 or 4. Thi is the best level to work at for running an exercise and will enable participants to understand the benefits of this technique.

2. Create an associated experience of having achieved that goal. What would you *see, hear, feel, taste* and *smell*? Be extravagant! Put everything that you can imagine into this representation. Feel it in your body—have big, bright, colourful pictures that are close to you. When you are satisfied that you have created a very desirable goal, move on.

3. Imagine you are holding your goal as you would a picture. Look at the picture. See yourself achieving that outcome. Make sure it is just as you would want it.

4 Imagine a line stretching in front of you out into your future. Notice how far along that line the goal belongs.

8. When you are back at now, look forward and see yourself achieving your outcome.

9. Relax and let go!

Part 4 (What if): Debrief—what do we get from this learning?

1. Collect reactions and feedback from the exercise. As before, go beyond like or dislike for the activity to what is learned about using the time line when working with goals?

2. How are the teachers feeling about their goals now? Do they seem more achievable, easier to accomplish and closer? What else do they notice about their goal?

3. How could this be applied in class, meetings or other areas of life?

Another great way to run this exercise is to do some well-formed outcome work first. Then the participants will have a really powerful goal to use on their time line. This is easy to do. Simply set it up as a coaching exercise and explain the importance of mental imagery to the achievement of outcomes. There is plenty on this in Chapter 2, *Blockbuster movies*. Below you can find a worksheet that is easy to use and which covers all the key areas.

Get the participants to work in pairs through the questions as coach and coachee.

Bird's eyeview: well formed outcome coaching

Asks well-formed outcome questions and records answers

Facilitator

You will need to allow about 20 minutes for each person, so this additional exercise will take about 40 minutes. You may also want to explore some of other time line tools in Chapter 12.

Questions to support the achievement of a well-formed outcome

To create a well-formed outcome, support the other person to develop positively phrased answers to the following questions. As you do so, ensure that you help them to see themselves having their outcome. Keep the language positive and future focused.

What specifically do you want?

What will having this do for you?

How will you know when you have achieved your outcome?

What will you see when you have achieved your outcome?

What will you hear when you have your outcome (both from your own internal dialogue and from others)?

What will you feel when you have your outcome?

Do you and you alone have control of your outcome?

Does your outcome involve others?

Can you both initiate and maintain the momentum to achieve your goal?	
When, where, how and with whom do you want this outcome?	
What will happen if you do achieve this outcome?	What will happen if you don't?
What won't happen if you do?	What won't happen if you don't?

Training exercise 6

The Walt Disney creativity strategy

(Estimated time needed: 40 minutes)

Part 1 (Why): Introduction—some possible questions to ask and ideas to introduce at the start

This is a fun activity that really gets people thinking. It is great also as an approach to lead into any school improvement planning or departmental action planning (as an icebreaker) as it helps people to understand the creative process. It works particularly well if you have already trained people in how to do spatial anchoring (or spotlighting).

- Have you ever had an idea? Have you ever had an idea and then found that when you shared it with someone else they just blocked it with a single comment?
- How would it be to understand what is going on and have a simple framework to support this?

Part 2 (What): Explanation—information we need to explain the NLP technique

This exercise does not appear elsewhere in the book. However, you should re-read Chapter 9, *Anchors away!* before you train this.

Robert Dilts, one of the early developers of NLP became very interested in creativity, so he decided to model one of the most creative people in the world, Walt Disney. He spent some time with Walt and discovered that he had an extraordinarily simple and powerful approach. He had three rooms that he used for his creative writing team. The rule was that each of these rooms was for a different stage in the storyboarding process. Room 1 was the dreamer's room. In this room all ideas were possible without limit. When Walt was in this room with his writers he only asked positive future-focused open questions (What else could we do? Any other ideas etc?). Room 2 was the realist room. Once all the possible ideas were out they all went into this room to bottom out how it was all to happen and think about what were the most realistic ideas—this was still a positive space with no critiquing yet allowed. Finally, they all went into a critique room to debate, discuss and challenge their ideas. Keeping these three stages of the creative process separate is a powerful way of ensuring that ideas flow and that they are achievable. As you do the exercise you will find that you have a preferred place. That's fine, all the places are equally important; it's all about getting a balance.

Part 3 (How): Activity—set up the exercise

This exercise has two parts. Firstly you need to get the audience to work in pairs to anchor three states to spaces on the floor. They can be marked with pieces of paper if you like.

Then the facilitator takes the participant through the exercise. The following activity sheet takes you through the process. We have found that it is helpful for some people to have the process written out before they do the activity.

Walt Disney creativity strategy

1. From the 'meta position' (or learning space) select three spaces in the floor and label them. You might like to write the words: Dreamer, Realist and Critic onto three pieces of paper.

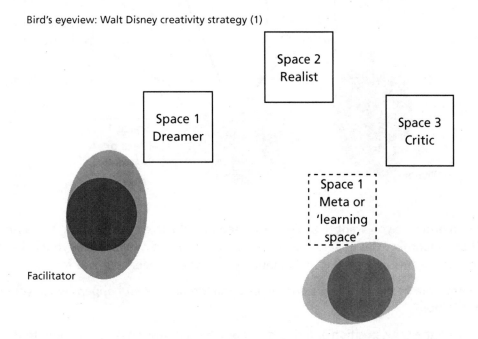

Bird's eyeview: Walt Disney creativity strategy (1)

2. First you need to 'anchor' the appropriate strategy to each physical location:

- Think of a time you were able to creatively dream up or fantasise new ideas without any limitations; step into the Dreamer location.

- Re-live that experience. What do you see, hear and feel?

- Step out of the space.

- Identify a time you were able to think very realistically and devise a specific plan to put an idea effectively into action; step into position 2 and re-live that experience. What do you see, hear and feel?

- Step out of the space.

- Think of a time you were able to constructively criticise a plan—that is, to offer positive and constructive criticism as well as to find problems. Make sure the location is far enough away from the others that it doesn't interfere. Step into location 3 and re-live that experience.

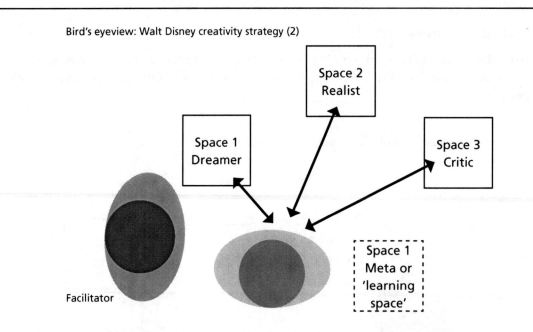

Bird's eyeview: Walt Disney creativity strategy (2)

3. Pick an outcome you want to achieve and step into the Dreamer location. Visualise yourself accomplishing this goal as if you were a character in a movie. Allow yourself to think about it in a free and uninhibited manner. What will you see, hear and feel?

4. Step into the Realist location, associate into the 'dream'. What happens when you adopt this position?

5. Step into the Critic position and find out if anything is missing or if you need to do something extra. Turn the criticisms into questions for the Dreamer.

6. Step back into the Dreamer position to creatively come up with solutions, alternatives and additions to address the questions posed by the Critic.

7. After you have repeated this cycle several times (you may want to swap around a bit) step into the 'Meta' or learning position. Feel yourself in the positions of all of the relevant characters. Then, see the process as if it were a storyboard (a sequence of images). What have you learnt?

8. Continue to cycle through Steps 4, 5 and 6 until your plan feels right and balanced for you. If you have a particular area that feels out of balance, or you just don't have enough of, simply step into the space and imagine a dial (like a volume control). Adjust the control until you have the feelings that you need. Remember this is about getting balance so no turning off the areas that are your least preferred ones. Often the greatest learning can come from the places that we least like to go.

Part 4 (What if): Debrief—what do we get from this learning?

1. Collect reactions and feedback from the exercise. As always, go beyond like or dislike for the activity to what is learned about how much information there is coming from people when they communicate, as most of it goes unnoticed.

2. What happened? What's changed for you now?

3. How could this be applied in class, meetings or other areas of life?

Expanding your repertoire by using the Puppet Master approach.

The Puppet Master approach is particularly useful for practising VAK language patterns, Satir categories, metaprograms and many other things. You may want to use it to help teachers be more flexible in responding to VAK language when dealing with parents. In this case, working in groups of three, two of the group sit or stand opposite one another taking on the role of teacher and parent. The third person is the Puppet Master and stands behind the teacher. The Puppet Master indicates (using cards or prearranged signals) V, A or K to the parent, who then adopts this language preference. The teacher must then respond to this, working to keep a high level of rapport so that the interaction remains positive. For a way of using this with Satir categories, see Toolbox No.15.

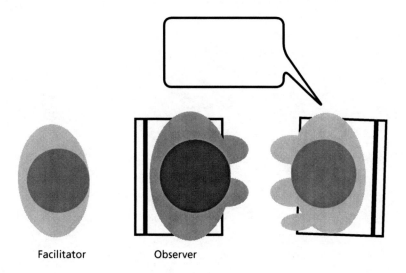

Facilitator   Observer

Always finish the exercise by debriefing what happened.

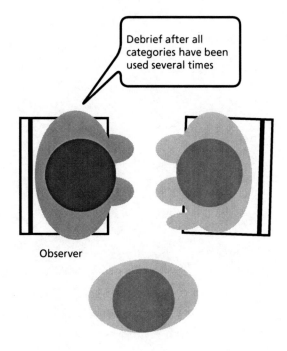

Observer

Glossary of commonly used NLP terms

Accessing cues

A term used when talking about the observation of body language and facial expressions. Accessing cues are subtle behaviours or micro-signals. These help to indicate how a person is thinking and feeling. Typical types of accessing cues include eye movements, voice tone, tempo, body posture, gestures and breathing patterns. Matching this sort of information is a key way to develop rapport.

Ambiguity

Ambiguity is the use of language which is vague or ambiguous. Ambiguous language is used in therapy as a form of waking hypnosis and can be used to create deeper trance. Using ambiguous language is one way of leading people through an influencing process.

Analogue

Having shades of meaning (i.e. on a continuum), as opposed to digital, which has a discrete (on/off) meaning. For example, in relation to submodalities (the subtle details of memory representations), something is either black and white or colour; however, brightness is a continuum from very light to completely dark.

Anchoring

The process by which an internal response is associated with an external trigger (similar to classical conditioning), so that the response may be quickly and sometimes covertly re-accessed. Anchoring can be visual (as with specific hand gestures), auditory (by using specific words and voice tone) or kinaesthetic (as when touching an arm or laying a hand on someone's shoulder).

Associated

In memory, when you appear to be looking through your own eyes, hearing what you heard and experiencing the feelings as if you were actually there. This is sometimes called an associated state.

Auditory

Relating to hearing or the sense of hearing.

Away from

Away from is a type of metaprogram. It is when a person's preference is to move in the opposite direction from what they don't want, as opposed to moving towards what they do want (e.g. *I don't want a 9 to 5 job*, as opposed to, *I want flexibility of hours*).

Beliefs

The generalisations we make about ourselves, others and the world. Beliefs act as self-fulfilling prophecies that influence all our behaviours. Beliefs are locked in place by the language we use to describe them—changing this language is an effective way to change limiting beliefs.

Break state

When someone 'breaks state' they suddenly interrupt their current physical and emotional state and are move to a different one. Typically, a break state is used to pull someone out of an unresourceful state into a neutral one, so that they are more easily able to do what is required to achieve their outcome. When using NLP therapeutic or personal development tools, a 'break state' is often used deliberately in order to ensure that the states being worked with are clearly separated from each other and therefore are 'clean'.

Calibration

The process of learning to read and interpret another person's unconscious, non-verbal responses and micro-signals.

Chunking

Organising, or breaking down, an experience into bigger or smaller pieces. Chunking up involves moving to a larger, more abstract level of information. Chunking down involves moving to a more specific and concrete level of information. Chunking laterally involves finding other examples at the same level of information. The term chunking is also applied to Milton and meta model language.

Congruence

When all of a person's internal beliefs, strategies and behaviours are fully in alignment and oriented towards securing a desired outcome they are said to have congruence.

Cross matching

Matching a person's body language with a different type of movement (e.g. tapping your foot in time to their speech rhythm).

Deep structure

The sensory maps (both conscious and unconscious) that people use to organise and guide their behaviour. In terms of language the deep structure is the meaning that is inherent in what has been said but which has not been stated.

Deletion

Within language, deletion is the process by which portions of the deep structure are removed and, therefore, do not appear in the surface structure representation (e.g. if someone were asked how they got to work and their reply was simply, *I caught the bus*, clearly a lot more happened; however, this information has been deleted). When this process occurs in relation to beliefs or outcomes, this can result in people omitting key information that they need in order to be more in touch with reality.

Digital

The opposite of analogue, see above.

Dissociated

In a memory when one appears to be looking at oneself, as if in a picture doing whatever you were doing, as opposed to seeing the event through your own eyes.

Distortion

In language where someone distorts what has happened or what is happening.

Down time

When a person's attention is inward, or when they are paying attention to their internal world and representations. Day dreaming is a form of down time.

Ecology

Ecology is the study of the consequences and effects of individual actions on the larger system. In NLP this same concept is applied to an individual. In other words, when carrying out changes or deciding on outcomes it is important to consider the whole life picture, including value, beliefs, etc.

Elicitation

The art of uncovering internal processes through questioning.

Eye accessing cues

Movements of the eyes in certain directions that may, through calibration, offer clues to people's inner thoughts, processing and feelings.

First position

See perceptual positions

Framing

To set a context or way of perceiving something upfront and, as a result of this, influence the outcome.

Future pacing

The process of mentally rehearsing and anchoring changes in yourself to a future imagined situation. This helps to ensure that the desired behaviour will occur naturally and automatically.

Generalisation

In language, generalisation is the process by which a specific experience comes to represent an entire category of experience. For example, *X always happens.*

Gustatory

Relating to the sense of taste.

Identity

Our sense of who we are. It is our sense of identity that informs our beliefs, capabilities and behaviours.

Installation

The process of facilitating the acquisition of a new strategy or behaviour.

Internal representation

Patterns of information we create and store in our minds as combinations of images, sounds, feelings, smells and tastes. Internal representations are the way we store and encode our memories in representational systems and their submodalities.

Kinaesthetic

Relating to body sensations. In NLP the term kinaesthetic is applied to all kinds of feelings including tactile, visceral and psychomotor.

Leading

Changing your own behaviours with enough rapport for the other person to follow. Effective leading is always preceded by pacing.

Matching

Adopting parts of another person's behaviour for the purpose of enhancing rapport.

Meta model

The model developed by John Grinder and Richard Bandler that identifies categories of language patterns. Meta model language chunks down into details to restore the generalisation, deletions and distortions in people's language and beliefs.

Metamessage

A message about a message. Your non-verbal behaviour is constantly giving people metamessages about you and the information you are providing. Sometimes these can contradict what you want to communicate.

Metaprogram

A level of mental programming that determines how we sort, orient to and chunk our experiences. These correlate to traits, preferences and schemata in applied psychology and cognitive neuroscience. We tend to behave according to our metaprograms and therefore we can be influenced by others matching them.

Milton model

Hypnotic language—specifically the language patterns of Milton Erickson. These work as the opposite of the meta model by chunking up out of detail into generalisations, distortions and deletions.

Mind reading

In NLP terms, this does not refer to the idea of telepathy, but rather to the assumptions that one sometimes makes about other people's thoughts or opinions.

Mirroring

Matching portions of another person's behaviour as if in a mirror.

Mismatching

Adopting different patterns of behaviour to another person, breaking rapport for the purpose of re-directing, interrupting or terminating a meeting or conversation.

Modelling

The process of observing and mapping the successful behaviours of other people in order to apply them to self and others.

Neurological levels of change

A practical model proposed by Robert Dilts for organising the elements of human experience. There are a number of tools that take people through these levels to help them to solve problems and feel more aligned in their life.

Olfactory

Relating to smell or the sense of smell.

Pacing

A method used to quickly establish rapport with people by matching certain aspects of their behaviour and/or experience. Pacing with language is a key part of the hypnotic process. Typically to influence, the pattern *pace, pace, lead* is required as a minimum.

Pacing current experience

This is the linguistic process of deliberately alluding to the present experience of another in order to pace and influence (e.g. *As you read these words …*)

Perceptual filters

Our unique combinations of values, beliefs, metaprograms, senses and language that shape our model of the world.

Perceptual position

A particular perspective or point of view. In NLP there are three basic positions one can take in perceiving a particular experience. First position involves experiencing something through our own eyes, associated in a first person point of view. Second position involves experiencing something as if we were in another person's shoes (in doing so the world would appear through the other person's eyes). Third position involves standing back and perceiving the relationship between ourselves and others objectively from a dissociated perspective.

Presupposition

An underlying assumption or meaning hidden in a sentence, as opposed to what it appears to say.

Rapport

The process of getting on with and trusted by another person. In NLP there are specific techniques for doing this. *See* cross matching, matching, mirroring, pacing.

Reframing

A linguistic process by which a person's current thinking is shifted by changing their point of view.

Representational systems

In NLP the term representational system applies to each of the five senses: seeing, hearing, touching (feeling), smelling and tasting.

Resources

Central to NLP is the notion that people have all the internal resources that they need. The word resource is therefore applied to anything that can support the achievement of an outcome: positive memories, internal emotional states, physiology, language patterns, etc.

Resourceful state

When a person feels emotionally resourceful and congruent.

Second position

See perceptual positions

Sensory acuity

The process of learning to make finer and more useful distinctions about the sense information we get from the world. One of the benefits that comes from studying NLP is the realisation that so much more is going on than we are normally aware of. Specifically, the term is often applied to the development of the awareness of facial and physiological micro-signals.

Spatial anchoring

This refers to the method of using physical location as an anchor for a specific behaviour.

Spotlighting

Using spatial anchoring in the classroom to influence group behaviour.

State

A person's state of mind and emotions at any moment in time.

Strategy

A set of explicit mental and behavioural steps used to achieve a specific outcome. The modelling of strategies is at the heart of NLP's study of excellence.

Submodalities

The subtle distinctions in perceptions, either visual, auditory, kinaesthetic, olfactory or gustatory. In a visual perception these might include whether the memory is colour or black and white, light or dark, etc.

Surface structure

The actual words someone uses. The opposite of deep structure, see above.

Swish pattern

A process by which visual internal representations are switched to facilitate changes in behaviour or to give more options.

Third position

See perceptual positions

Time line

The internal representation of memories on a chronological line.

Trance

When our conscious experience appears to be an altered state of consciousness, e.g. day dreaming. Trance can be induced by a range of processes including hypnotic language or just open questioning.

Transderivational search for meaning (TDS)

The process of locating meaning by going into a trance.

Uptime

This is the opposite of downtime, and means when the individual is paying attention to what is going on external to them, in their environment, and not to their internal processes.

Values

In NLP the term values is applied to those things that are important to you—not objects or people, but rather experiences/feelings such as learning, health, wisdom, respect. They are the non-physical qualities that we seek to have more of in our life.

Visual

Relating to sight or the sense of sight.

Well-formed outcome

A well-formed outcome is an outcome that is: positively stated, under the person's control, right-sized and ecological to their values, beliefs and life conditions.

References

Altmann, G. T. M. (2004) Language-mediated eye movements in the absence of a visual world: the 'blank screen paradigm', *Cognition*, 93: B79–B87

Altmann, G. T. M. and Kamide, Y. (2004) Now you see it, now you don't: mediating the mapping between language and the visual world, in J. M. Henderson and F. Ferreira (eds), *The Interface of Language, Vision, and Action: Eye Movements and the Visual World*, New York: Psychology Press

Andersen, R. A., Essick, G. K. and Seigal, R. M. (1985) Encoding of spatial location by posterior parietal neurons, *Science*, 230: 456–458

Antonakis, J. (2003) Why 'emotional intelligence' does not predict leadership effectiveness: a comment on Prati, Douglas, Ferris, Ammeter, and Buckley, *International Journal of Organizational Analysis*, 11: 4: 355–361

Atkinson, D. (2004) Theorising how student teachers form their identities in initial teacher education, *British Education Research Journal*, 30: 3: 379–394

Avenanti, A., Paluello, L. M., Bufalari, I. and Aglioti, S. M. (2006). Stimulus-driven modulation of motor-evoked potentials during observation of others' pain, *Neuroimage*, 32: 1: 316–324

Baddeley, M. and Predebon, J. (1991) Do the eyes have it?: a test of neurolinguistic programming's eye-movement hypothesis, *Australian Journal of Clinical Hypnotherapy and Hypnosis*, 12: 1: 1–23

Bandler, R. (1985) *Using Your Brain for a change*, Moab, UT: Real People Press

Bandler, R. and Grinder, J. (1975a) *The Structure of Magic I: A Book about Language and Therapy*, Palo Alto, CA: Science and Behaviour Books

Bandler, R. and Grinder, J. (1975b) *Patterns of the Hypnotic Techniques of Milton H. Erickson, M.D.* vol. i, Cupertino, CA: Meta Publications

Bandler, R. and Grinder, J. (1975c) *Patterns of the Hypnotic Techniques of Milton Erickson, M.D.* vol. ii, Cupertino, CA: Meta Publications

Bandler, R. and Grinder, J. (1976a) *Patterns of the Hypnotic Techniques of Milton H. Erickson, M.D.* vol ii. Cupertino, CA: Meta Publications

Bandler, R. and Grinder, J. (1976b) *The Structure of Magic II*, Palo Alto, CA: Science and Behaviour Books

Bandler, R. and Grinder, J. (1979) *Frogs into Princes*, Moab, UT: Real People Press

Bandler, R. and MacDonald, W. (1988) *An Insider's Guide to Sub-modalities*, Cupertino, CA: Meta Publications

Bar-On, R. (1997) *Bar-On Emotional Quotient Inventory (EQ-I): Technical Manual.* Toronto, Canada: Multi-Health Systems

Bar-On, R. (2000) Emotional and social intelligence: insights from the emotion quotient inventory, in R. Bar-On and J. Parker (eds), *The Handbook of Emotional Intelligence*, San Francisco: Jossey-Bass

Baron, J. (2000) *Thinking and Deciding*, New York: Cambridge University Press

Bateson, G. (1972) *Steps to an Ecology of Mind*, London: Paladin, Granada

Bechara A., Damasio H. and Damasio, A. R. (2000) Emotion, decision making and the orbitofrontal cortex, *Cerebral Cortex*, 10: 295–307

Bechara A., Damasio H., Damasio, A. R. and Lee, G. P. (1999) Different contributions of the human amygdala and ventromedial prefrontal cortex to decision-making, *Journal of Neuroscience*, 19: 5473–5481

Bechara A., Tranel D., Damasio H. and Damasio A. (1996) Failure to respond automatically to anticipated future outcomes following damage to prefrontal cortex, *Cerebral Cortex*, 6: 215–225

Benzwie, T. (1987) *A Moving Experience*, Tucson, AZ: Zephyr Press

Berne, E. (1964) *Games People Play*, New York: Grove Press

Birdwhistell, R.L. (1970) *Kinetics and Context: Essays on Bodily-Motion Communication*, Philadelphia: University of Pennsylvania Press

Blakemore, S.-J. And Frith, U. (2007) *The Learning Brain*, London: Blackwell

Boddenhamer, B. G. and Hall, L. (2003a) *The User's Manual for the Brain*, vol. i: *The Complete Manual for Neuro-linguistic Programming Practitioner Certification*, Carmarthen: Crown House

Boddenhamer, B. G. and Hall, L.(2003b) *The User's Manual for the Brain*, vol. ii: *Mastering Systemic NLP*, Carmarthen: Crown House

Boussaoud, D. and Bremmer, F. (1999) Gaze effects in the cerebral cortex: reference frames for space coding and action, *Experimental Brain Research*, 128: 170–180

Bower, B. (2005) Goal-oriented brain cells: neurons may track action as a prelude to empathy, *Science News*, April 30

Brandt, S. A. and Stark, L. W. (1997) Spontaneous eye movements during visual imagery reflect the content of the visual scene, *Journal of Cognitive Neuroscience*, 9: 27–38

Briere, J. and Scott, C. (2006) *Principles of Trauma Therapy: A Guide to Symptoms, Evaluation, and Treatment*, Thousand Oaks, CA: Sage

Brophy, J. (1981) Teacher praise: a functional analysis, *Review of Educational Research*, Spring, 5–32

Brophy, J. E. and Good, T. L. (1986) Teacher behaviour and student achievement, in M.C. Wittock (ed.), *Handbook of research on teaching*, New York: Macmillan, 328–375

Brown, R. J. and Oakley, D. A. (2004) An integrated cognitive theory of hypnosis and high hypnotizability, in M. Heap, R. J. Brown and D. A. Oakley (eds), *The Highly Hypnotisable Person: Theoretical, Experimental and Clinical Issues*, London: Routledge

Buckner, M., Meara, N. M., Reese, E. J. and Reese, M. (1987) Eye movement as an indicator of sensory components in thought, *Journal of Counseling Psychology*, 34: 3: 283–287

Buzan, T. (2001) *Mind Maps at Work: How to be the Best at Work and Still Have Time to Play*, London: Harper Collins

Carr, L., Iacoboni, M., Dubeau, M.-C., Mazziotta, J. C. and Lenzi, G. L. (2003) Neural mechanisms of empathy in humans: a relay from neural systems for imitation to limbic areas, *Proceedings of the National Academy of Science*, 100: 5497–5502

Cavanna, A. E. and Trimble, M. R. (2006) The precuneus: a review of its functional anatomy and behavioural correlates, *Brain*, 129: 564–583

Chomsky, N. (1957) *Syntactic structure*, The Hague: Mouton

Churches, R. and Terry, R. (2005) Streetwise body language. *Teaching Expertise*, 10: 50–51

Churches, R. and Terry, R. (2006a) Don't think about chocolate cake: an introduction to influential language patterns, *Teaching Expertise*, 11: 15–16

Churches, R. and Terry, R. (2006b) Feng Shui in the classroom, *Teaching Expertise*, 12: 22–24

Churches, R and Terry, R. (2006c) You can do it and it's about time, *Teaching Expertise*, 13: 25–27

Claxton, G. (2002) *Building Learning Power*, Bristol: TLO Limited

Coffield, F., Moseley, D., Hall, E. and Ecclestone, K. (2004a) *Learning Styles and Pedagogy—in Post 16 Learning: A Systematic and Critical Review*, London: Learning and Skills Research Centre, Institute of Education

Coffield, F., Moseley, D., Hall, E. and Ecclestone, K. (2004b) *Should We Be Using Learning Styles? What Research Has to Say to Practice*, London: Learning and Skills Research Centre, Institute of Education

Craft, A. (2001) Neuro-linguistic programming and learning theory, *The Curriculum Journal*, 12: 1: 125–136

Craik, F. I. M. and Lockhart, R. S. (1972) Levels of processing: a framework for memory research, *Journal of Verbal Learning and Verbal Behavior*, 11: 671–684

Croft, W. (1998) Linguistic evidence and mental representations, *Cognitive Linguistics*, 7: 151–173

Damasio, A. R. (1994) *Descartes' Error: Emotion, Rationality and the Human Brain,* New York: Putnam

Damasio, A. (2000) *The Feeling of What Happens: Body, Emotion and the Making of Consciousness,* London: Vintage

Dapretto, M., Davies, M. S., Pfeifer, J. H., Scott, A. A., Sigman, M., Bookheimer, S. Y. and Iacoboni, M. (2006) Understanding emotions in others: mirror neuron dysfunction in children with autism spectrum disorders, *Nature Neuroscience*, 9: 1: 28–30

Darwin, C. (1872) *The Expression of Emotions in Man and Animals,* London: John Murray

Davidson, P. R. and Parker, K. C. H. (2001) Eye movement desensitization and reprocessing (EMDR): a meta-analysis, *Journal of Consulting and Clinical Psychology*, 69: 2: 305–316

Davis, J. (1988) *On Matching Teaching Approach with Student Learning Style: Are We Asking the Right Question?* Memphis, TN: University of Memphis

De Souza, J. F. X., Dukelow, S. P., Gati, J. S., Menon, R. S., Andersen, R. A. and Vilis, T. (2000) Eye position signal modulates a human parietal pointing region during memory-guided movements, *Journal of Neuroscience*, 20: 15: 5835–5840

Dijksterhuis, A. and Smith, P (2002) Affective habituation: subliminal exposure to extreme stimuli decreases their extremity, *Emotion*, 2: 203–214

Dilts, R. and Epstein, T. (1995) *Dynamic Learning*, California: Meta, Capitola

Dilts, R., Grinder, J., Bandler, R., Delozier, J. (1980) *Neuro-linguistic Programming: The Study of the Structure of Subjective Experience*, Cupertino, CA: Meta Publications

Dragovic, T. (2007) *Teachers' Professional Identity and the Role of CPD in its Creation—A Report on a Study into how NLP and Non-NLP Trained Teachers in Slovenia Talk about their Professional Identity and their Work*, International Society for Teacher Education, 27th Annual International Seminar at University of Stirling, Scotland, 24–30 June

Druckman, D. and Swets, J. (1988) *Enhancing Human Performance*, Washington, DC: National Academy Press

Dunn, R., Dunn, K. and Price, G. E. (1984) *Learning Style Inventory,* Lawrence, KS: Price Systems

Ekman, P. (1985) *Telling Lies: Clues to Deceit in the Marketplace, Politics and Marriage,* New York: Morton

Ekman, P. (2003) *Emotions Revealed*, London: Phoenix

Eriksson, P. S., Perfilieva, E., Björk-Eriksson, T., Alborn, A.-M., Nordborg, C., Peterson, D. and Gage, F. (1998) Neurogenesis in the adult human hippocampus, *Nature Medicine* 4, 1313–1317

Eysenck, H. (2000) *Intelligence: A New Look*, Brunswick, NJ: Transaction Publishers

Fauconnier, G. (1994) *Mental Spaces, Aspects of Meaning Construction in Natural Language,* Cambridge: Cambridge University Press

Fauconnier, G. (1997) *Mappings in Thought and Language,* Cambridge: Cambridge University Press

Faymonville, M. E., Boly, M. and Laueys, S. (2006) Functional neuroanatomy of the hypnotic state, *Journal of Physiology*, 99: 463–469

Fogassi, L., Ferrari, P. F., Gesierich, B., Rozzi, S., Chersi, F. and Rizzolatti, G. (2005) Parietal lobe: from action organization to intention understanding, *Science,* 308: 662–667

Freedman, J. L. and Fraser, S. C. (1966) Compliance without pressure: the foot-in-the-door-technique, *Journal of Personality and Social Psychology*, 4: 2: 195–202

Fullan, M. (2001) *Leading in a Culture of Change*, San Francisco: Jossey-Bass

Fullan, M. (2003) *The Moral Imperative of School Leadership*, Thousand Oaks, CA: Corwin Press

Fullan, M. (2005) *Leadership and Sustainability: System Thinkers in Action*, Thousand Oaks, CA: Corwin Press

Fullan, M. (2007) Leading in a system of change, Paper prepared for Conference on Systems Thinking and Sustainable School Development, Utrecht, February, OISE/University of Toronto

Gagne, R.M., Yekovick, C.W. and Yekovich, F.R. (1993) *The Cognitive Psychology of School Learning*, New York, HarperCollins

Gallese, V., Fadiga, L., Fogassi, L. and Rizzolatti, G. (1996) Action recognition in the premotor cortex, *Brain*, 119: 2: 593–609

Gallese, V., and Goldman, A. (1998) Mirror neurons and the simulation theory of mindreading, *Trends in Cognitive Sciences*, 2: 493–501

Gallese, V., Keysers, C. and Rizzolatti, G. (2004) A unifying view of the basis of social cognition, *Trends in Cognitive Sciences*, 8: 9: 396–403

Garner, I. (2000) Problems and inconsistencies with Kolb's learning styles. *Educational Psychology: An International Journal of Experimental Educational Psychology*, 20: 3: 341–348

Gentili, R., Papaxanthis, C. and Pozzo, T. (2005) Improvement and generalisation of arm motor performance through motor imaginary practice, *Neuroscience*, 137: 3: 761–772

Gilmore, D. T., Maischein, H.-M. and Nusslein-Volhard, C. (2002) Migration and function of a glial bubtype in the vertebrate peripheral nervous system, *Neuron*, 43: 577–588

Gilovich, T. (1993) *How We Know What Isn't So: The Fallibility of Human Reason in Everyday Life*, New York: The Free Press

Ginott, H. G. (1972) *Teacher and Child: A Book for Parents and Teachers*, London: Macmillan

Gluck, M. A., Meeter, M. and Myers, C. E. (2003) Computational models of the hippocampal region: linking incremental learning and episodic memory, *Trends in Cognitive Sciences*, 7: 6: 269–276

Goldberg, M. E., Colby, C. L., Duhamel, J. R. (1990) Representation of visuomotor space in the parietal lobe of the monkey, *Cold Spring Harbor Symposia on Quantitative Biology*, 55: 729–739

Goleman, D. (1995) *Emotional Intelligence*, New York: Bantam Books

Goleman, D. (1996) *Emotional Intelligence: Why It Can Matter More Than IQ*, London: Bloomsbury

Goleman, D. (2001) Emotional intelligence: issues in paradigm building, in C. Cherniss

and D. Goleman (eds), *The Emotionally Intelligent Workplace*, San Francisco: Jossey-Bass

Goleman, D. (2006) *Social Intelligence*, London: Hutchinson

Grinder, J. and Bandler, R. (1981) *Trance-formations*, Moab, UT: Real People Press

Grinder, J. and Elgin, S. (1973) *Guide to Transformational Grammar*, New York: Holt, Rinehart and Winston

Gruzelier, J. (1998) A working model of the neurophysiology of hypnosis: a review of evidence, *Contemporary Hypnosis*, 15: 1: 9–21

Gruzelier, J. (2006) Frontal functions, connectivity and neural efficiency underpinning hypnosis and hypnotic susceptibility, *Contemporary Hypnosis*, 23: 1: 15–32

Guay, F., Marsh, H. W. and Bovin, M. (2003) Academic self-concept and academic achievement: developmental perspectives on their causal ordering, *Journal of Educational Psychology*, 95; 1: 124–136

Gudmundsdottir, S. (1990) Values in pedagogical content knowledge, *Journal of Teacher Education*, 41: 3: 44–52

Haesler, S., Wada, K., Nshdejan, A., Morrisey, E. E., Lints, T., Jarvis, E. D. and Scharff, C. (2004) FOXP2 expression in avian vocal learners and non-learners, *Journal of Neuroscience*, 24: 13: 3164–3157

Hafting, T., Fyhn, M., Molden, S., Moser, M.-B. and Moser, E. I. (2005) Microstructure of a spatial map in the entorhinal cortex, *Nature*, 436: 801–806

Halligan, P. W. and Oakley. D. A. (2000) Greatest myth of all, *New Scientist*, 168: 35–49

Hargreaves, D. (2005) *About Learning: Report of the Learning Working Group*, London: Demos

Harris, M. J. and Rosenthal, R. (1985) Mediation of interpersonal expectancy effects: 31 meta-analyses, *Psychological Bulletin*, 97: 363–386

Harrison, N. A., Singer, T., Rotshtein, P., Dolan, R. J., and Critchley, H. D. (2006) Pupillary contagion: central mechanisms engaged in sadness processing, *SCAN*, 1: 5–17

Heap, M., Brown, R. J. and Oakley, D. A. (2004) *The Highly Hypnotizable Person: Theoretical, Experimental and Clinical issues*, London: Routledge

Hebb, D. O. (1968) Concerning imagery, *Psychological Review*, 75: 466–477

Higgins, S., Wall, K., Hall, E., Baumfield, V., Leat, D., Moseley, D. and Woolner, P. (2007) *Learning to Learn in Schools: Phase 3, Final Report*, Campaign for Learning, University of Durham, University of Newcastle and the Institute of Education, London University

Hilgard, E. R. (1974) Towards a neo-dissociationist theory: multiple cognitive controls in human functioning, *Perspectives in Biology and Medicine*, 17: 301–316

Johansson, R., Holsanova, J. and Homqvist, K. (2006) Pictures and spoken descriptions elicit similar eye movements during mental imagery, both in light and in complete darkness, *Cognitive Science*, 30: 6: 1053–1079

Kalisch, R., Wiech, K., Critchley, H. D., Seymour, B., O'Doherty, J. P., Oakley, D. A, Allen, P. and Dolan, R. J. (2005) Anxiety reduction though detachment: subjective, physiological, and neural effects, *Journal of Cognitive Neuroscience*, 17: 6: 874–883

Kamin, L. J. (1968) 'Attention-like' processes in classical conditioning, in M. R. Jones (ed.), *Miami Symposium on the Prediction of Behavior: Aversive Stimulation*, Miami: University of Miami Press, 9–33

Kayser, C. (2007) Listening with your eyes, *Scientific American Mind*, 18: 2: 24–29

Kayser, C., Petkov, M., Augart, N. and Logothetis, N. (2005) Integration of touch and sound in auditory cortex, *Neuron*, 48: 2: 373–384

Keysers, C., Wicker, B., Gazzola, V., Anton, J. L., Fogassi, L., and Gallese, V. (2004) A touching sight: SII/PV activation during the observation and experience of touch, *Neuron*, 42: 2: 335–346

Kirsch, I (1977) Suggestibility or hypnosis: what do our scales really measure? *International Journal of Clinical and Experimental Hypnosis*, 45: 212–225

Kirsch, I., Lynn, S. J., Vigorito, M. and Miller, R. R. (2004) The role of cognition in classical and operant conditioning, *Journal of Clinical Psychology*, 60: 369–392

Knierim, J. J. (2007) The matrix in your head, *Scientific American Mind*, 18: 3: 42

Knight, K. (1990) Effects of learning style accommodation on achievement of second graders, Paper presented at the meeting of the Mid-South Educational Research Association, New Orleans, November

Kolb, D. A. (1995) The process of experiential learning, in M. Thorpe, R. Edwards and A. Hanson (eds) *Culture and Processes of Adult Learning*, Milton Keynes: Open University

Korthagen, F. A. J. (2004) In search of the essence of a good teacher, *Teaching and Teacher Education*, 20: 1: 77–97

Korzybski, A. (1933, 1994) *Science and Sanity: An Introduction to Non-Aristotelian Systems and General Semantics*, Lakeville, CT: The International Non-Aristotelian Library Publishing Company

Kosslyn, S. M. (1996) *Image and Brain*, Cambridge, MA: MIT Press

Laborde, G. Z. (1983) *Influencing With integrity*, Palo Alto, CA: Syntony

Laeng, B. and Teodorescu, D. S. (2002) Eye scanpaths during visual imagery reenact those of perception of the same visual scene, *Cognitive Science*, 26: 207–231

Leithwood, K., Day, C., Sammons, P., Harris, A. and Hopkins, D. (2006) *Seven Strong Claims About Successful School Leadership*, Nottingham: National College for School Leadership

Lopez, J. C. (2000) Shaky memories in indelible ink, *Nature Reviews Neuroscience*, 1: 6–7

Lubow, R. E. and Moore, A. U. (1959) Latent inhibition: the effect of non-reinforced preexposure to the conditional stimulus, *Journal of Comparative and Physiological Psychology*, 52: 415–419

Lucas, B. (2001) *Power Up Your Mind: Learn Faster, Work Smarter*, London: Nicholas Brearley Publishing

McCarthy, B. (1981) *The 4Mat System: Teaching to Learning Styles with Right/Left mode Techniques*, Illinois: Excel

Macaluso, E. and Driver, J. (2005) Multisensory spatial interactions: a window into functional integration in the human brain, *Trends in Neurosciences*, 28: 5: 264–271

Maquet, P., Faymonville, M. A., Degueldre, C., Delfiore, G., Franck, G., Luxen, A. and Lamy, M. (1999) Functional neuroanatomy of hypnotic state, *Biological Psychiatry*, 45: 327–333

Marcus, G. F. and Fisher, S. E. (2003) FOXP2 in focus: what can genes tell us about speech and language? *Trends in Cognitive Sciences*, 7: 6: 257–262

Marr, D. (1971) Simple memory: a theory for archicortex, *Philosophical Transactions of the Royal Society of London, Series B, Biological Sciences,* 262: 841: 23–81

Marsh, H. W., Hau, K.-T. and Kong, C.-K. (2002) Multilevel causal ordering of academic self-concept and achievement: influence of language of instruction (English compared with Chinese) for Hong Kong Students, *American Educational Research Journal,* 39: 3: 727–763

Mather, M., Shafir, E. and Johnson, M. K. (2000) Misrememberance of options past: source monitoring and choice, *Psychological Science,* 11: 132–138

Mathison, J. (2006) *Phenomenology,* Surrey University, Centre for Management Learning and Development <http://www.nlpresearch.org>

Mathison, J. (2007) *Mirror Neurons: A Neurological Basis for Making Sense of the Words, Feelings and Actions of Others,* Surrey University, Centre for Management Learning and Development <http://www.nlpresearch.org>

Mayer, J. (2005) *Can Emotional Knowledge Be Improved? Can You Raise Emotional Intelligence?* University of New Hampshire http://www.unh.edu/emotional_intelligence/ accessed 2 January 2006

Mehrabian, A. (1971) *Silent Messages,* Belmont, CA: Wadsworth

Mehrabian, A. (1972) *Nonverbal Communication,* Chicago, IL: Aldine-Atherton

Mehrabian, A. (1981) *Silent Messages: Implicit Communication of Emotions and Attitudes,* Belmont, CA: Wadsworth

Miller, G. (1956) The magical number seven plus or minus two: some limits on our capacity to process information, *Psychological Review:* 63; 81–97

Miller, G. A., Galanter, E. and Pribram, K. (1960) *Plans and the Structure of Behaviour,* New York: Holt Rhinehart and Winston

Miller, R. R. and Matzel, L. D. (2000) Memory involves far more than 'consolidation', *Nature Reviews Neuroscience:* 1: 214–216

Mortimore, P., Sammons, P., Stoll, L., Lewis, D. and Ecob, R. (1988) *School Matters,* Somerset Wells: Open Books

Mortimore, P., Sammons, P., Stoll, L., Lewis, D. and Ecob, R. (1988) *School Matters,* Wesport, CT: Praeger

Muijis, R. D. (1998) The reciprocal relationship between self-concept and school achievement, *British Journal of Educational Psychology,* 67: 3: 263–277

Muijis, R. D. and Reynolds, D. (1999) School effectiveness and teacher effectiveness: some preliminary findings from the evaluation of the mathematics enhancement programme, Paper presented at the American Education Research Association Conference, Quebec, Montreal, 9 April

Muijis, R. D. and Reynolds, D. (2005) (2nd edn) *Effective Teaching, Evidence and Practice,* London: Sage

Myers, I. B. (1995) *Gifts Differing: Understanding Personality Type,* California: Mountain View

Nakahara, K. and Miyashita, Y. (2005) Understanding intentions: through the looking glass, *Science,* 308: 644–645

Neck, C. P. and Manz. C. C. (1992) Thought self-leadership: the influence of self-talk and mental imagery on performance, *Journal of Organizational Behavior,* 13: 7: 681–699

Norman, D. A. and Shallice, T. (1986) Attention to action: willed and automatic control of behaviour, in R. J. Davidson, G. E. Swartz and D. Shapiro (eds), *Consciousness and Self-regulation: Advances in Research and Theory,* New York: Plenum, 1–18,

Nottebohm, F., O'Loughlin, B., Gould, K., Yohay, K. and Alvarez-Buylla, A. (1994) The life span of new neurons in a song control nucleus of the adult canary brain depends on time of year when these cells are born, *Proceedings of the National Academy of Sciences,* 91: 7849–7853

Oberman, L. M., Hubbard, E. M., McCleery, J. P., Altschuler, E. L., Ramachandran, V. S. and Pineda, J. A. (2005) EEG evidence for mirror neuron dysfunction in autism spectrum disorders, *Cognitive Brain Research,* 24: 190–198

Öhman, A. and Soares, J. J. F. (1994) Unconscious anxiety: phobic responses to masked stimuli, *Journal of Abnormal Psychology,* 103: 231–240

O'Keefe, J. and Nadel, L. (1978) The hippocampus as a cognitive map http://www.cognitivemap.net accessed 7 July 2007

Pachler, N., Daly, C. and Lambert, D. (2003) Teacher learning: reconceptualising the relationship between theory and practical teaching in master's level course development, *Proceedings: Forum for Quality Assurance in Distance-Learning,* University of London: Institute of Education

Pascual-Leone, A., Nguyet, D., Cohen, L. G., Brasil-Neto, J. P., Cammarota, A. and Hallett, M. (1995) Modulation of muscle responses evoked by transcranial magnetic stimulation during the acquisition of new fine motor skills, *Journal of Neuroscience,* 74: 3: 1037–1045

Patrizi, F. M. (1982) Self-attitude enhancement through positive mental imagery, Paper presented at the 90th Annual Convention of the American Psychological Association

Pavlov, I. (1927) *Conditioned Reflexes,* London: Oxford University Press

Perls, F., Hefferline, R.F. and Goodman, P. (1951) *Gestalt Therapy: Excitement and Growth in the Human Personality,* London: Souvenir Press

Perls, F. (1951) *Gestalt Therapy: Excitement and Growth in the Human Personality Verbatim,* Moab, London: Souvenir

Ramachandran, V. S. (2006) Mirror neurons and imitation learning as the driving force behind 'the great leap forward' in human evolution, *Edge Foundation* <http://www.edge.org> accessed June 2007

Ramachandra, V.S. and Oberman, L. M. (2007) Broken mirrors: a theory of autism, *Scientific American Reports, Special Edition on Child Development,* 17: 2: 20–29

Rescorla, R. A. (1969) Conditioned inhibition of fear resulting from negative CS-US contingencies, *Journal of Comparative and Physiological Psychology,* 67: 504–509

Restorff, H. von (1933). Über die wirkung von bereichsbildungen im spurenfeld (The effects of field formation in the trace field), *Psychologie Forschung,* 18: 299–34

Reynolds (1992) School effectiveness and school improvement: an updated review of the British literature, in D. Reynolds and P. Cuttance (eds) *School Effectiveness: Research, Policy and Practice,* London: Cassell

Richardson, D. C. and Dale R. (2005) Looking to understand: the coupling between speakers' and listeners' eye movements and its relationship to discourse comprehension, *Cognitive Science,* 29: 6: 1045–1060

Richardson, D. C. and Spivey, M. J. (2000) Representation, space and Hollywood squares: looking at things that aren't there anymore, *Cognition,* 76: 269–295

Rizzolatti, G., Fadiga, L., Gallese, L. and Fogassi, L. (1996) Premotor cortex and the recognition of motor actions, *Cognitive Brain Research,* 3: 131–141

Rizzolatti, G., Fogassi, L. and V. Gallese, V. (2001) Neurophysiological mechanisms underlying the understanding and imitation of action, *Neuroscience,* 2: 661–670

Roberts, R. D., Zeidner, M., and Matthews, G. (2001) Does emotional intelligence meet traditional standards for an intelligence? Some new data and conclusions, *Emotion*, 1: 3: 196–231

Rogers, C. R. (1959) A theory of therapy, personality and interpersonal relationships, as developed in the client-centered framework, in S. Koch (ed.), *Psychology: A Study of Science*, 210–211

Rosen, S. (1982) *My Voice Will Go With You: The Teaching Tales of Milton H. Erickson*, New York: Norton

Rosenshine, B. and Furst, N. (1973) The use of direct observation to study teaching, in R. W. M. Travers (ed.), *Second Handbook of Research on Teaching*, Chicago: Rand McNally

Rosenthal, R. and Ambady, N. (1993) Half a minute: predicting teacher evaluations from thin slices of nonverbal behaviour and physical attractiveness, *Journal of Personality and Social Psychology*, 64: 3: 443–441

Rowe, M. B. (1986) Wait time: slowing down may be a way of speeding up, *Journal of Teacher Education*, 80: 4: 206–211

Sargolini, F., Fyhn, M., Hafting, T., McNaughton, L., Witter, M. P., Moser, M.-B. and Moser, E. I. (2006) Conjunctive representation of position, direction and velocity in entorhinal cortex, *Science*, 312: 758–762

Satir, V. (1967) *Conjoint Family Therapy: A Guide to Theory and Technique*, Palo Alto, CA: Science and Behavior Books

Satir, V. (1972) *Peoplemaking*, Palo Alto, CA: Science and Behavior Books

Satir, V. (1988) *The New Peoplemaking*, Palo Alto, CA: Science and Behavior Books

Servan-Schreiber, D. (2002) Eye movement desensitization and reprocessing: is psychiatry missing the point? *Psychiatric Times*, 14: 7: 36–40

Shapiro, F. (1995) *Eye Movement Desensitization and Reprocessing: Basic Principles, Protocols and Procedures*, New York: The Guilford Press

Skinner, B. F. (1974) *About Behaviourism*, New York: Longman

Smith, A. (2000) *Accelerated Learning in Practice: Brain-based Methods for Accelerating Motivation and Achievement*, Stafford: Network Educational Press

Smith, A (2002) *The Brain's Behind It*, Stafford: Network Educational Press

Smith, A. (2003) *Accelerated Learning: A User's Guide*, Stafford: Network Educational Press

Smith, A. and Call, N. (1999) *The ALPS Approach: Accelerated Learning in Primary Schools*, Stafford: Network Educational Press

Smith, M.C. (1968) CS-US interval and US intensity in classical conditioning of the rabbit's nictitating membrane response, *Journal of Comparative and Physiological Psychology*, 66: 679–687

Stahl, S. A. (2002) Different strokes for different folks? in L. Abbeduto (ed.), *Taking Sides: Clashing on Controversial Issues in Educational Psychology*, Guilford, CT: McGraw-Hill, 98–107

Stickgold, R., Hobson, J. A., Fosse, R. and Fosse, M. (2001) Sleep, learning and dreams: off-line memory reprocessing, *Science*, 294: 5544: 1053–1057

Sweeney, J. A., Luna, B., Keedy, S. K., McDowell, J. E. and Clementz, B. A. (2007) fMRI studies of eye movement control: investigating the interaction of cognitive and senorimotor brain systems, *Neuroimage*, 36: 54–60

Taylor, J. A. and Shaw, D. F. (2002) The effects of outcome imagery on golf-putting performance, *Journal of Sports Sciences*, 20: 8: 607–613

Tettamanti, M., Buccino, M., Saccuman, M. C., Gallese, V., Danna, M., Scifo, P., Fazio, F., Rizzolatti, G., Cappa, S. and Perani, D. (2005) Listening to action-related sentences activates fronto-parietal motor circuits", *Journal of Cognitive Neuroscience* 17: 2: 273–281

Thorndike, E. L. (1901) Animal intelligence: an experimental study of the associative processes in animals, *Psychological Review Monograph Supplement*, 2: 1–109

TLRP (2007) *Neuroscience and Education: Issues and Opportunities*, Economic and Social Research Council

Tognoli, E., Lagarde, J., De Guzman, G. C. and Scott Kelso, J. A. (2007) The phi complex as a neuromarker of human social coordination, *Proceedings of the National Academy of Science*, 104: 19: 8190–8195

Tosey, P. (2006) *An Annotated Index of NLP Terms in Bandler and Grinder's Early Publications*, University of Surrey, Centre for Management Learning and Development <http://www.nlpresearch.org> accessed 25 July 2007

Tosey, P. and Mathison, J. (2003a) Neuro-linguistic programming and learning theory: a response, *Curriculum Journal*, 14: 3: 371–388

Tosey, P. and Mathison, J. (2003b) Neuro-linguistic programming: its potential for learning and teaching in formal education, Paper presented at the European Conference on Educational Research, University of Hamburg, 17–20 September

Tosey, P. and Mathison, J. (2007) Fabulous creatures of HRD: a critical natural history of neuro-linguistic programming, Paper for the Eighth International Conference on HRD Research and Practice Across Europe, Oxford Brookes Business School, 27–29 June

Tosey, P., Mathison, J. and Michelli, D. (2005) The potential of neuro-linguistic programming, *Journal of Transformative Education*, 3: 2: 140–167

Velmans, M. (2000) *Understanding Consciousness*, London: Routledge

Vignemont, F. de and Singer, T. (2006) The empathic brain: how, when and why? *Trends in Cognitive Sciences*, 10: 10: 435–441

Wagner, A. R., Logan, F. A., Haberlandt, K. and Price, T. (1968) Stimulus selection in animal discrimination learning, *Journal of Experimental Psychology*, 76: 171–180

West-Burnham, J. (2002) *Leadership and spirituality*, NCSL Leading Edge Seminar Thinkpiece

West-Burnham, J. (2004) Leadership and personal effectiveness, Paper written for a seminar at the Royal Garden Hotel, London, November, Nottingham: National College for School Leadership

West-Burnham, J. and Huws Jones, V. (2007) *Educating for Understanding: Spiritual and Moral Development in Schools*, London: Network Continuum Press

West-Burnham, J. and Ireson, J. (2005) *Leadership Development and Personal Effectiveness*, Nottingham: National College for School Leadership

Wicker, B., Keysers, C., Plailly, J., Royet, J.-P., Gallese, V. and Rizzolatti, G. (2003) Both of us disgusted in my insula: the common neural basis of seeing and feeling disgust, *Neuron*: 40: 655–644

Wiener, N. (1961) *Cybernetics*, New York: John Wiley and Sons

Wilson, D., Silver, S. M., Covi, W. G. and Foster, S. (1996) Eye movement desensitization and reprocessing: effectiveness and autonomic correlates, *Journal of Behavior Therapy and Experimental Psychiatry*, 27: 3: 219–229

Wirth, S., Yanike, M., Frank, L. M., Smith, A. C., Brown, E. N. and Suzuki, W. A. (2003) Single neurons in the monkey hippocampus and learning of new associations, *Science*, 300: 1578–1581

Woolfolk, R. L., Parrish, M. W. and Murphy, S. M. (1985) The effects of positive and negative imagery on motor skill performance, *Journal of Cognitive Therapy and Research*, 9: 3: 335–341

Zeineh, M. M., Engel, S. A., Thompson, P. M. and Book-heimer, S. Y. (2003) Dynamics of the hippocampus during encoding and retrieval of face-name pairs, *Science*, 299: 577–580

Zipser, D. and Andersen, R. A. (1988) A back-propagation programmed network that simulates response properties of a subset of posterior parietal neurons, *Nature*, 331: 679–684

A chronological bibliography of key texts in relation to the development and publication of NLP

Bandler, R. and Grinder, J. (1975a) *The Structure of Magic: A Book about Language and Therapy*, vol. i, Palo Alto, CA: Science and Behaviour Books

Deep and surface language structure

Distortion

Deletion

Generalisation

Eye movement model

Meta model language

Predicates

Presuppositions

Bandler, R. and Grinder, J. (1975b) *Patterns of the Hypnotic Techniques of Milton Erickson, M.D.* vol. i, Cupertino, CA: Meta Publications

Milton model

Modelling

Primary experience and secondary experience

Bandler, R. and Grinder, J. (1975c) *Patterns of the Hypnotic Techniques of Milton Erickson, M.D.* vol. ii, Cupertino, CA: Meta Publications

Congruence

Lead system

Transderivational search

Bandler, R. and Grinder J. (1976) *The Structure of Magic II: A Book about Communication and Change,* Palo Alto, CA: Science and Behaviour Books

Addition of digital representation system

Congruence

Incongruence

Input channels

Meta model

Representational system

Satir categories of communication

Russell's Theory of Logical Type (application of)

Bandler, R., Grinder, J. and Satir, V. (1976) *Changing with Families: A Book about Further Education for Being Human,* Palo Alto, CA: Science and Behaviour Books

Meta model

Satir categories

Representational systems

Bandler, R. and Grinder, J. (1979) *Reframing,* Moab, UT: Real People Press

Reframing

Bandler, R. and Grinder, J. (1979) *Frogs into Princes,* Moab, UT: Real People Press

Accessing cues

'All communication is hypnosis'

Anchoring

Change personal history

Dissociation patterns

Ecology

Eye movement model and relationship to representational system

Flexibility of behaviour

Future pacing

Mirroring

Pacing and leading

Perceptual positions

Phobia cure

Polarity response

Rapport

Reframing

Strategy

Transderivational search

Dilts, R., Grinder, J., Bandler, R., Bandler, L. C. and Delozier, J. (1980) *Neuro-linguistic Programming: The Study of the Structure of Subjective Experience,* CA: Meta Publications

Definition of NLP as the study of the structure of subjective experience

Grinder, J. and Bandler, R. (1981) *Trance-formations,* Moab, UT: Real People Press

NLP training approaches to hypnosis and waking state hypnosis

Bandler, R. (1985) *Using Your Brain for a change,* Moab, UT: Real People Press
    Submodalities

Bandler, R. and MacDonald, W. (1988) *An Insider's Guide to Sub-modalities,* Cupertino, CA: Meta Publications
    Submodalities

For a fully annotated index of NLP terms in Bandler and Grinder's early publications see Tosey (2006) http://www.nlpresearch.org accessed 25 July 2007

List of NLP Toolboxes

Index

Biographies

Richard Churches

Richard Churches is Principal Consultant for National Programmes at CfBT Education Trust, the world leading education consultancy. In recent years he has worked on a number of major UK government initiatives for the DfES and the National College for School Leadership. This has included being the national lead consultant for Fast Track teaching, Managing Editor for the NPQH materials and consultant for the London Leadership Strategy. He is currently National Programme Manager for the support materials for the new secondary curriculum. Richard was an Advanced Skills Teacher in Greenwich and before that held senior management posts in two inner London schools. He has taught in primary and secondary phases and in a special school. He is reading for a PhD at Surrey University School of Management and is a Fellow of the RSA.

Roger Terry

Roger Terry is an International NLP Master Trainer and public speaker. As an expert on Neuro-linguistic Programming and human value systems Roger leads seminars and consults with organisations in the UK, USA, Europe and Middle East. He is the author of *The Hidden Art of Interviewing: NLP and Qualitative Research.* His published articles include regular contributions to *Teaching Expertise* magazine with Richard Churches. Roger has, with Henrie Liddiard, trained over 1,000 Fast Track teachers in NLP. Eleven years ago he founded Evolution Training with his wife and business partner Emily. Previously his career was within the utility sector where he was responsible for new business creation and innovative organisational development. He now works with organisations and individuals, guiding them to evolve to their full potential.

Lightning Source UK Ltd.
Milton Keynes UK
UKOW03f1914181214

243345UK00003B/33/P